WILD WATERS

Canoeing North America's Wilderness Rivers

WILD WATERS

Canoeing North America's Wilderness Rivers

Edited by JAMES RAFFAN
Foreword by BILL MASON

FIREFLY BOOKS

A FIREFLY BOOK

Cataloguing in Publication Data

Main entry under title:

Wild waters

Rev. ed.
ISBN 1-55209-132-5

1. Canoes and canoeing – Canada. 2. Wild and scenic rivers – Canada.
3. Canada – Description and travel. I. Raffan, James.

GV776.15.A2W55   1997   917.104'647   C96-93296-8

Firefly Books (U.S.) Inc.
P.O. Box 1338, Ellicot Station
Buffalo, New York 14205

Printed and bound in Hong Kong

97 98 99 00 6 5 4 3 2 1

Contents

*To the native people who showed us
these rivers that we call wild*

Foreword to Second Edition

BY JAMES RAFFAN

In the decade since the original publication of this volume, awareness of the plight of our wild rivers has risen exponentially and, although there is much work left to be done to ensure that this precious North American resource is shared and protected in a sustainable way, there is modest reason for celebration as well. In Canada, the Canadian Heritage Rivers System is gaining strength, notoriety, and respect, and in the United States the legislative shield of the Wild and Scenic Rivers Act is being buoyed and bolstered daily by an increasing number of governmental and non-governmental advocacy groups, conservation organizations, and private citizens prepared to *act* to find ways to ensure that pristine river experiences will be available for future generations. This collection of photographs and essays, which now includes chapters featuring an Alaskan river and a river in the continental United States, is meant to illuminate the stunning riparian beauty of this continent that is our home and to underline the hope that its readers will get involved in the preservation and sensible use of all our natural resources, especially rivers, first locally, then regionally, nationally, and internationally. But as any paddler and conservationist will tell you, the most effective environmental action is that which is informed by first-hand experience on the land itself. For those who cannot access the rivers, for whatever reason, these first-hand accounts constitute the next best thing to actually feeling the spray and splendor of the rivers themselves; but for those who can walk a riverbank or paddle a boat, these photographs and essays are meant to get the juices flowing, to fire the imagination, to move you to dust off the old rowboat and get out there. See you on the river.

James Raffan
Seeley's Bay, Ontario
October 1996

Foreword

BY BILL MASON

In a lifetime of canoeing you couldn't paddle all the rivers of North America. You could hardly paddle all the major rivers, let alone the thousands of obscure little wilderness rivers that have rarely seen a canoe. I get depressed just thinking about all those rivers that I will never see. One problem is that when I fall in love with a river, such as the Petawawa, the Pukaskwa, or the Nahanni, I've got to see it again and again. I've actually worn a groove down the middle of the Petawawa I've run it so many times. I could spend a lifetime on the Nahanni and never satisfy my curiosity about all those feeder streams and the rivers that flow into it out of hidden valleys. I long to know what's up there. So what do you do? Even if you lived to a hundred you're not going to see even a fraction of them.

I've heard it said, "You see one river, you've seen them all." But that's like walking into the Louvre and saying, "You see one picture, you've seen them all!" Each river is a personality. A good contour map of a river is like a portrait. It gives you a picture of the temperament you can expect from it. Some rivers are young and boisterous, some old and rather grand in their bearing. Some rivers are totally unpredictable. They flow through so many types of terrain that you never know what to expect. There are rivers that will bore you one minute and kill you the next. It takes a while really to get to know them.

Half the fun of being a canoeist is sharing a river with friends. You can take them with you or tell them about it or show them your slides. I have had a glorious time sharing my love of rivers through films that I have made, and now I do it through painting. Books are probably one of the best ways to share a river because the reader can experience it again and again. With a book you have instant recall. I appreciate those who have shared their rivers with me: I feel as though I have caught a glimpse of that river's personality. Often it will convince me to go and see it for myself. Knowing what to expect can heighten the joy of anticipation that all canoeists experience before a trip.

There is always a fear that over-popularizing a river will destroy its wilderness character. This is a real and legitimate concern, for it has happened to many rivers. However, a natural outgrowth of falling in love with a river is a concern for its well-being, its health and wild character. This in turn leads—or should lead—to one more voice speaking up for its preservation. I've always felt that a river is much more than a place to go to have fun. A river is a living being that can speak to the soul or the spirit. Wild rivers are an endangered species. They are being lost at an alarming rate, gobbled up by our industrial world. But we are not only physical beings: the spiritual part of us is just as important. I might never get to many or most of those rivers, but knowing they are out there, wild and free, fills me with anticipation and excitement.

This book is a means of sharing some of the rivers that have spoken to us. We hope they will speak to you.

I did not envy Jim Raffan's job of narrowing the selection to fit between these covers—this book should have been several feet thick—but I believe he has chosen well. I can think of no one better to set the guidelines for this book and to pull together the diversified talents of the canoeists found herein. Jim is a skilled white-water instructor, wilderness guide and expert on wilderness medicine. What impresses me most about Jim Raffan, though, is his concern for wild places and for the animals and plants that live there; and he has chosen writers who share his concern. We are only visitors, part of these wild places for a while. And we are so much richer for having been there, whether in person or in books such as this.

Overleaf: *Gilded by the coming of fall, aspens in the Nahanni River's First Canyon stand out against forest and cliff.*

Greenland

Baffin Bay

Baffin Island

Legend

....

● National capitals

State and provincial capitals

⌃ State and provincial boundaries

〜 *Rivers*

〜 *Rivers featured in text*

Labrador Sea

Atlantic Ocean

George R.

Hudson Bay

LABRADOR

Severn R.

La Grande R.

Pipestone R.

Attawapiskat R.

Manicouagan R.

Moisie R.

St. John's

NEWFOUNDLAND

Gulf of St. Lawrence

ONTARIO

QUEBEC

Missinaibi R.

Nipigon R.

Charlottetown

NEW BRUNSWICK

Quebec

Lake Superior

Nipissing R.

Fredericton

NOVA SCOTIA

Halifax

MAINE

Ottawa ●

VERMONT

Augusta

MICHIGAN

Lake Huron

Montpelier

NEW HAMPSHIRE

WISCONSIN

Lake Michigan

Muskegon R.

Toronto

Lake Ontario

Connecticut R.

Concord

Madison

Lansing

Albany

Boston

NEW YORK

MASSACHUSETTS

Hartford

RHODE ISLAND

CONNECTICUT

Lake Erie

PENNSYLVANIA

NEW JERSEY

The challenge of white water lures paddlers to North America's wild rivers. Shooting the rapids of the Nahanni's notorious "Rock Garden," this crew, like all river adventurers, must balance exhilaration and thrills with good sense and safety.

International River Classification Scale

Reference is made in this volume to the International River Classification Scale, which is used by white-water paddlers to categorize rapid difficulty.

I   Moving water with a few riffles and small waves; no obstructions.

II   Easy rapids with waves up to 3 feet. Channels are wide and obvious without scouting. Some maneuvering necessary.

III   Rapids with high, irregular waves that could swamp an open canoe. Narrow passages require scouting and complex maneuvering.

IV   Long and difficult rapids with constricted passages that often require precise maneuvering in turbulent water. Scouting from shore is often necessary and conditions make rescue difficult. Generally impossible for open canoes.

V   Extremely difficult, long, and very violent rapids. Complicated routes must be scouted from shore. Significant hazard to life in event of mishap.

VI   Difficulties of Class V carried to the extreme of navigability. Nearly impossible and very dangerous for closed canoes. Serious risk to life.

It is accepted practice to consider rapids one class more difficult in cold or extreme-wilderness conditions. This scale is for paddler reference only. Ratings change with river water levels.

Wild river canoeing—passport to a North American dream. In insect country, a repellent-soaked bug jacket or "citronella negligée" is a must, especially when winds are calm.

CHAPTER ONE

Our Wild Rivers

This book is a celebration of North America's wild rivers. It features eight expedition-length rivers, which encompass the rich diversity of North America's wild-river heritage. The rivers were selected not because they are wilder or more scenic or cleaner than wilderness water courses close to home, but in order to permit a number of seasoned wilderness travelers to share their distinctive ways of valuing the river experience. From the rain-washed Moisie in the east, to the turbid Bonnet Plume in the west, come experience adventures on remote and dangerous rivers, some protected, others not. But first, explore the quintessential North American river experience and see that these wild rivers are a diminishing resource whose continued existence will not come without the work and commitment of North Americans from every part of the continent.

Wild But Not Free

BY JAMES RAFFAN

It saddens me that the wild-river valley where I grew up is now under water. In truth, the Speed River north of Guelph, Ontario—"the mighty Speed" we called it—was no more wild than your average Holstein. But along its banks, in a riverside corridor where farmers couldn't plow, willows hung over fish-twitching pools, and tangled thickets made a boy's wilderness.

With an unquenchable spirit of adventure, I'd wander up the river to places that nobody else knew about, past the spot where a flood-control dam now squats, and into territory that, I was sure, was just short of the North Pole. Using logs and bits of wood ripped loose by spring ice, I'd build a raft and drift home, late for supper and usually very wet. I was Christopher Columbus, Huck Finn, Captain Hook, and Guy the Voyageur. Or just a kid, wondering who fed the ducks and where the water came from.

The rafts were replaced by summer-camp canoes, and my life expanded to include other streams and other adventures. I'm sure that nothing has had greater effect on my view of the world than a long succession of river expeditions that began so simply, so close to home. Surviving wild northern waters and harsh weather bred self-reliance. Being swayed by the power of swollen rivers and wilderness led to my feeling comfortable separate from the trappings of home. The stories, memories, and river-deep friendships that grew out of these experiences have richly colored my life.

But shortly after I graduated from university in biology, an arctic river reopened my eyes. Standing on the barren shores of the Coppermine River, overwhelmed by black-flies and mosquitoes, I felt, for the first time, like a visitor in a river world. Fear of a forbidding place forced me to attend to the river in a way I had never done before. It taught me that fish don't need fish ladders if there are no dams. It taught me that human emotion confounds our understanding of the relationship of wolf and caribou. And it taught me that, without barriers, only caution prevents slipping over the brink. I learned what wild really means.

The real joy of river travel comes from exploring the total river environment. On the Coppermine River, "Rocknest," a prominent hill near its source, gives a remarkable overview of the mighty river.

With my head crammed with scientific exactitudes, it took the Coppermine River community to show me that nature does not revolve around human interests. I saw budding horns of a uniquely human

Coppermine white water—a test of team work and skill. The removable spray cover widens safety margins in rough, cold (46°F) northern waters. Caribou antlers on board make an awkward yet memorable souvenir.

dilemma: I was awed by things wild, yet I knew that just by being there I interrupted the flow of nature. I had to conclude that the only meaningful way to view the world was not through my own eyes but from some distant hill, seeing myself as just one element in a much larger scheme. I also saw the canoe as the perfect vehicle for a peaceful resolution of the dilemma. In it I could be part of nature.

At the same time I made new connections to history. Around quiet campfires on the Coppermine, smoke from gnarled wood tweaked our imaginations as we talked of native people and read from the journals of Samuel Hearne and Sir John Franklin. Like never before I felt part of our Canadian past. I realized that the river routes that reticulate this land from sea to arctic sea bear the very essence of who we are. By paddling the Coppermine, stripped of school and its interpreters, I was experiencing the land much as Hearne, Franklin, and its native custodians had left it centuries earlier. Reason enough, I thought, to treasure the river.

Indeed, many lives have been changed, for better and for worse, by capricious northern waters. River adventures give us new eyes, new ways of looking at the world, sometimes immediate, sometimes latent, and often in a transferable, metaphorical way. John Kauffman has contemplated the "mysterious element to the ever-changing changelessness of flowing water. Rivers prompt us to ask where from, where to, how deep, and what is around the bend?" In 1909, Agnes Laut wrote, "It is a curious sensation, canoeing down a vast river whose waters sweep an area equal to half a dozen European kingdoms and at every bend reveal shifting vistas of new peoples and new regions." Contributing author Bob Henderson speaks of a "strange freedom surfaced in this primitive setting, in activity, materials, and desire linked so closely with the land." And back-country philosopher Willi Unsoeld described the meaning of a wilderness experience as "a renewal exercise that leads to a process of alteration. You go to nature for your metaphysical fix— your reassurance that the world makes sense. It's a reassurance that there's something behind it all and it's good."

There are those to whom metaphysical notions are as foreign as traveling the same route twice. They crash down northern streams just to collect river names like so many stuffed lion heads. "River baggers," as they've been called, miss the real river experience.

Other paddlers would keep wild rivers secret. Yet, the "ever-changing

changelessness" of a river, which makes *every* river experience unique, and gives people this desire to keep secrets, is the same trait that allows paddlers to be explorers again and again, discovering the invisible trails of their predecessors and leaving no tracks.

There are still others, bureaucrats who relate to rivers through statistics. They insist that rivers of cultural or ecological significance should be catalogued, rivers of big vertical drop and constant flow should be dammed, and urban rivers should be used to dilute wastes to acceptable levels.

We all have our favorite river close to home, but more and more expedition-quality wild rivers now figure in the designs of paddlers, rafters, politicians, and technocrats. This leaves me naggingly questioning why the existence of these priceless communities must be rationalized in the human context. Why must wild rivers justify their undammed, undeveloped state? Is it too much to ask that a river be left alone for its own sake?

Unfortunately, the answer is yes. In countless head-to-head battles between economics and ecology, rivers have lost. In the human world, in which the laws of economics overrule laws of nature, we may have to put barriers around the precious parts of our river heritage to even the odds.

If we do so, we should acknowledge three things. We must recognize that parks in themselves are paradoxical: protective barriers mean increased use. Second, because such barriers tend to constrict the natural evolution of a river, we must enclose tracts of land large enough to allow the river community—not the park—to dominate. And most important, we must acknowledge that recreational, commercial,

Lying back in a canoe being swept along at 6 miles per hour, a paddler gets an unusual view. Even without the swallows and birds of prey that make riverside cliffs home, rocky crags on the Coppermine River have a beauty of their own.

and government river users must cooperate! The alternative is the Ottawa River, voyageur highway to the west. Once wild, it will not be wild again, at least not in this ice age.

We know how to live in harmony with nature: we can clean water before we put it back in the rivers; we can tap and process mineral resources without scarring the landscape; and we can utilize natural power sources without compromising every river valley in the country. But whether what we *can* do becomes what we *will* do is largely dependent on how many people adopt a new way of looking at our rivers.

This view may mean that boaters will have to stand in line for the privilege of paddling popular wild rivers. It may mean that regulated promotion of increased river use will be seen as a necessary and useful tradeoff for increased awareness, appreciation, and advocacy; because there is no substitute for actually having been *on* a wild river when it comes to speaking up for preservation. It may mean ecologists and industrialists will have to focus on their similarities and not on their indignations. A new river view may mean that we will have to issue permits for river use, as the Americans do.

The major rivers in our primary drainage basins—Columbia in the Pacific, Mackenzie in the Arctic, Nelson flowing to Hudson Bay, St. Lawrence in the Atlantic basin, Mississippi and Rio Grande heading south to the Gulf—are heavily exploited, and development schemes metastasize. Inhospitable geography has protected most of our wild rivers and will probably continue to do so, because travel is difficult in the mountains and high on the Canadian Shield. Yet it is increasingly possible to manage large tracts of river land by remote control. Witness the Churchill River in Labrador and the La Grande in Quebec: beyond civilization, we thought, but today they are dammed and silent.

In the 1950s Thomas W. Kierans came up with an idea to create a sea-level, dike-enclosed freshwater lake within James Bay from which water would be channeled to southern markets. His proposal still gets attention. Protecting our wild rivers from such maniacal schemes might best be done through legislated wilderness, a profound contradiction. It makes sense to cordon off significant wild areas, and it's naïve to think that anything less will have lasting effect. If one day a united consciousness narrows the gap between environmental understanding and environmental degradation, we can take the fences down; meanwhile, we need laws to keep our wild rivers wild.

Evening camp: mirrored images of tree and cloud play on still waters while a tired crew reflects on a rich river day. It's time for setting up tents, preparing a fireside supper, and reliving the day's highlights.

The Americans passed the Wild and Scenic Rivers Act in 1968; and we recently established the Canadian Heritage Rivers System, an initiative involving all levels of government in the protection of our valuable rivers. Under the system, our rivers are evaluated on their merits, not solely on whether they advance human development plans. It's a big step in the right direction, and the scheme is working!

Rivers are at the very heart of this continent. Without them, who would we be? We must preserve them, and to do that we must take effective, united—and informed—action. At stake is an irreplaceable treasure that is very much a part of who we are. In *Why We Act Like Canadians* Pierre Berton put it this way:

> ...we are a nation of canoeists, and have been since the earliest days, paddling our way up the St. Lawrence, across the lakes, over the portages of the Shield, west along the North Saskatchewan through the Yellowhead gap and thence southwest by the Columbia and Fraser rivers to the sea. When somebody asks you how Canada could exist as a horizontal country with its plains and mountains running vertically, tell him about the paddlers.

And while you're at it, like the authors of the following fine river tales which now include stories of rivers in Alaska and the continental United States—Mason, Franks, Henderson, Harrison, Schaber, Gaskin, Usher, and Allan—tell him about the rivers, the wild rivers of North America.

The quality of light is one of the most compelling features of the northern landscape. Below, *canoeists paddle into shimmering water under rapidly lowering skies;* at bottom, *canoes glide silently through still water under a midnight sun; and,* below right, *the sun's rays draw water into the clouds from the deserted lake.*

Wild river cliffs provide important nesting habitat for large carnivorous birds. Viewed in early August from a photographer's makeshift blind, this fledgling golden eagle on the Coppermine River must learn to fly and hunt in the few weeks before the snow flies.

Racing to the Gulf of St. Lawrence in a deep glacial valley through the rugged eastern edge of the Canadian Shield, the Moisie River is one of eastern Canada's most spectacular and challenging for canoeists.

CHAPTER TWO

Eastern Wild

The eastern edge of the Canadian Shield is a forbidding wilderness, but through the centuries this land of deep river valleys, rain, and mosquitoes has engendered a strange fascination in the adventuresome few. Winter and summer, rugged individuals are drawn to such rivers as the George, Wheeler, and Whale, which flow into Ungava Bay; the Ugjoktok, Churchill, and Kanairiktok, which run through Labrador to the Atlantic, and the Little Mecatina, Natashquan, and Romaine, which flow from the highlands of Labrador to Quebec's North Shore. Perhaps the best-known and most-traveled eastern river, the one of greatest volume on the North Shore, is the Moisie. It rises in Lake Opocopa near the Labrador border and flows 260 miles south to the Gulf of St. Lawrence near Sept-Iles, Quebec.

Moisie: Nahanni of the East

BY FRED GASKIN

Four modern-day voyageurs arrive in Labrador City with paddles, packs, and provisions for a two-week descent of Moisie River. All components for the expedition are accounted for except the two canoes, which, having arrived in advance, are locked up in a warehouse, location unknown! It is also Regatta Day, a festival of summer games when the only signs of life were at the airport and the local bar. Our sole option is to leave the airport and begin our canoe search at the hotel.

The sympathetic woman bartender and local patrons systematically eliminate all storage possibilities until a phone call produces information as to the likely whereabouts of the local freight manager. He found the canoes in a locked warehouse within sight of the pre-trip watering hole. Kit complete, it is now possible to arrange our transport into the Labrador wilderness.

The Moisie, known to the Montagnais Indians as the "Mis-te-shipu," or Great River, is most often approached by crossing the height of land from Labrador. We had paddled together on many journeys in northern Ontario, the Northwest Territories, and western Quebec, but Ingo Schoppel, Robbert Hartog, Jack Purchase, and I were looking forward to our first major Quebec/Labrador wilderness river.

Unfortunately, we acted on poor advice and flew from Sept-Iles to Labrador City, thereby missing the opportunity of traveling north on the legendary Quebec North Shore and Labrador Railway. While trying to locate our errant canoes, we learned at the bar that, despite reduced iron-mining operations in the interior, the QNS&L remains the best—and cheapest—way to gain access to the Moisie. It would have been a great ground-level preview of the Moisie lands.

Senses tingle to the fresh, damp smell of morning mist.

So we wouldn't be totally deprived of rail transport, we rode the late evening "Cottage Run," west from Labrador City to our put-in on Lac De Mille, 19 miles east of town. We had our own boxcar for canoes and gear, and spent the hour as guests of the trainmen in the locomotive. These would prove the most relaxing 19 miles of our two-week trip.

At 11:00 p.m. the train stopped, we bade farewell to our generous hosts and paddled to an island, where we set up camp—a camp that became home for

Early in its tempestuous run to the sea, the Moisie is joined by the Pekans River at this foaming confluence. The Pekans drops 459 feet in the 6 miles immediately upstream from the Moisie.

Two members of author Gaskin's crew line a loaded canoe through a side channel on the Moisie. The risk of the canoe upsetting and being lost downriver makes team work as important in this river maneuver as it is in paddling white water.

Running the rapids gives canoeists the ultimate sensation of exhilaration and achievement.

The danger of spilling makes flotation devices mandatory.

two and a half days while heavy winds whipped the lake. Fortunately, the weather moderated sufficiently by noon of the third day to permit us to cross Lac De Mille and ascend a creek to the portage over the height of land that took us into Quebec and to the headwaters of the Moisie River. We camped in an area devastated by forest fire and, it seemed, prone to natural disasters: we were sent rushing for the shelter of the tent after supper that night by a shower of marble-sized hailstones.

The following day, we were somewhat tense as we paddled across Lac Menistouc and Lac Opocopa and entered the Moisie. From here we would descend 260 miles to the gulf, running and portaging each day's ration of the challenging rapids we had heard so much about.

In addition to topographic maps, we had excellent information from "Gens Du Nord" of Sept-Iles to help us through the rapids. From experience with other such notes we knew that changing water levels tend to make these descriptions notoriously unreliable. Yet their annotated trip maps were flawless, and their rapid classifications on the international white-water scale were completely accurate. We concluded that the water levels in the year the notes were made were identical to ours in 1983. The notes were in French, but once we related the word cordelle to the process of lining, they saved us time and contributed to our success in completing the trip without a single upset.

No written description, however, can replace paddling expertise, experience, and good equipment. We had two 18-foot Old Town ABS voyageur canoes complete with deck covers, and were able to handle all Class III rapids with comparative safety. In conjunction with the Gens Du Nord maps, we defined Class IV rapids as having a "30% chance of upset," and Class V as "upset inevitable." Spray covers or not, we portaged many times a day, day after day!

An evening paddle—alone with still water, setting sun, and an empty canoe that seems to enjoy a load-free frolic.

The lower part of our descent of the Moisie River would retrace the historic canoe route of Henry Youle Hind, who, in 1861, became the first European to explore this part of Quebec and Labrador. We had with us a copy of Hind's journal, which gave us opportunities to compare experiences of the rapids and canyons of the lower Moisie.

Our objectives were challenge, adventure, and recreation; but Hind, a professor of geology at the University of Toronto, was intent on mapping the Moisie and exploring the interior, in the hope of giving Labrador a place in the

Moisie rapids present a great variety of challenges for white-water paddlers. Depending on a group's skill, most river sections can be run; others should be lined or portaged. The relatively uniform gradient of the Moisie makes it one of the greatest sources for Atlantic salmon. For waterfowl, however, the swift current makes the Moisie an unpopular river for raising young.

Below: *Rain and mist continually haunt the Moisie River.*

future of British North America. He had with him five French-Canadian voyageurs, two Indian guides, two government surveyors, and his brother William, who went along as expedition artist (a usual requirement until the advent of the camera). On June 10, 1861, they began struggling upstream on the Moisie River against a current still swollen with spring runoff; they returned, one month later, whisked south by the many rapids of the Moisie.

We got many a taste of what Hind was up against. Halfway down one rapid, I spotted a portage. Ingo and I quickly stopped our descent, walked the canoe across ledges and rocks, and pulled into a well-used trail. Realizing that the portage was worn for good reason, we grabbed loose ropes and ran along the shore to provide whatever assistance we could to Robbert and Jack, who had missed the turn.

They were lodged on the rocks on the wrong side of the river just above a place where it dropped almost 100 feet straight down through a succession of falls. Careful upstream tracking and a tenuous river crossing reunited our party for the mile-long canyon portage. Frequent shore vantage points provided ample opportunity to appreciate and photograph the awesome beauty of the canyon and its crushing white water. We had often been told about spectacular white-water canoeing in Quebec and Labrador: without question, the Moisie upholds this reputation!

Another major portage took us to the massive cascades at the confluence of the Pekans River and the Moisie. The lively white water at the foot of the falls provided Ingo with six speckled trout in short order. In addition to the speckles, the frying pans contained sliced mushrooms, collected along the portage. Lunch, that day, was off the land.

Some canoeists use the Pekans River to approach the Moisie. This trip begins with road rather than rail transport out of Labrador City, but the proportion of portaging to canoeing on the Pekans is far greater, and its arrival at the Moisie is heralded by a 2-mile portage. As we feasted on fresh trout and mushrooms, we studied the Pekans and concluded that our route was amply tough to satisfy our sense of adventure.

All the portaging and the possibility of severe weather forced us to spend long hours on the river to ensure that we would make it to Sept-Iles on the Labor Day weekend, within our two-week time limit. But this eight-to-nine-hour-a-day paddling schedule was suspended without hesitation on what was to be our only rain-free day of the entire journey. It was one of those warm,

Kitchen with a view.

sunny days typical of northern Ontario river trips. We discovered a short but beautiful cascade broken by large rock islands spanning the river. We camped early in glorious sunshine and took a long-awaited and highly enjoyable rest.

Robbert took on the duties of innkeeper and commenced preparations for a gourmet wilderness dinner, while Ingo endeavored to fulfill a promise to provide speckled trout *hors d'oeuvres*. Jack and I set out to capture the beauty of the site on film and to prove it is possible to have a bath in the Moisie's icy water.

On our rock-island home, we found many scour holes—perfectly cylindrical cavities in the rock worn smooth by ice and water—as deep as a man and 6 feet wide. So intent were we in our inspection of this phenomenon that I fell into a hole hidden by foliage. Numerous scrapes, but thankfully no broken bones! With assistance from Jack, I limped back to camp in time for supper. The arrival of a crippled colleague evoked no sympathy, just concern that three able-bodied voyageurs were being set up to do the portaging for four!

A bad leg didn't preclude paddling and enjoying this canyoned river some call "the Nahanni of the east." It was exciting to hold back and watch Jack and Robbert proceed through the turbulence with an unerring instinct, disappearing in the trough and returning to view farther on, all with optimum daring, tempered with an equivalent measure of safety. Our own descent would follow, retracing the route of the lead canoe or charting a new course, but with the same sensation of exhilaration and achievement.

At one point, the river narrowed to a dark 32-foot gap and drove through a short canyon. Deathly silent black water coursed between the rock walls, its smoothness broken only by miniature whirlpools that erupted and vanished. It was a strange and mystical sensation drifting through the canyon on a river unexpectedly silent, only a fraction of its normal width, but possibly a hundred times its usual depth.

Periodically the slopes of the river valley were punctuated with sparkling streams that cascaded hundreds of feet from the valley crest. They seemed to swell with every passing day.

To our chagrin, intermittent daily rains turned into a continuous downpour that seemed to last for days. We broke camp in the rain, portaged and paddled in the rain, ate lunch in the rain, and, paddling, looked in vain—in the rain— for our next campsite.

The low point of the trip was at eight o'clock on the evening we arrived at

Although summer temperatures are a comfortable 55–60°F, fog and drizzle occur frequently in the Moisie valley. In July and August, monthly precipitation averages around 4 inches, with measurable rainfall occurring on about 40% of summer days. Lack of campsites in the dense, wet forest forces tenters onto riverside rock, where the ground is flat and bugs are fewer.

Fish Ladder portage, a grotty spot that would have to be home for four rain-soaked, chilled paddlers. There was barely adequate space for the tent. The temperature was falling toward freezing; and Ingo's uncontrollable shaking underlined the urgency of providing shelter, fire, and warm, dry clothes. It was a frightening reminder of our fallibility. Two hours later, with spirits restored, we drank a rum toast to our arrival and survival.

When the sun's welcome rays penetrated the water-soaked forest, I was overwhelmed by one benefit of all this moisture. There were luxuriant mosses everywhere, as much as 3 feet deep, which have built up over the years; moss so thick that very little undergrowth develops in the northern Quebec rain forest. This moss made me appreciate rain, for the only time on the trip.

While paddling down the lower Moisie wilderness, we frequently noted evidence of three important Quebec resources: a salmon fishing lodge; the iron-ore trains of the QNS&L railroad along the river; and in the far distance, hydro towers crossing the horizons with power for rural and urban communities.

This gradual return to civilization retraced Hind's homeward journey on the Moisie. It was at Hind's "fifth rapid" (second from the mouth of the Moisie River) that we decided to end our trip. Rather than run the rapid and risk a "50% chance of an upset," and to shorten the trip by 16 miles, we pulled out at the QNS&L railroad bridge over the Moisie. Hind was right when he described "a steep and slippery mountain path—straight up!" It was quite a climb to get away from the river; fortunately, all our portaging had prepared us.

There was no one at the railroad maintenance building and no telephone; however, we were fortunate to encounter one of the locals, who offered to take Robbert into town on his dirt bike to arrange for collecting our station wagon. Awaiting his return, as dusk was falling, three fatigued but contented voyageurs watched an ore train cross the bridge and disappear into a tunnel on its way to Sept-Iles. Like us, it was full of the riches of the north, and destined for the south.

Fred Gaskin's lifetime list of river expeditions reads like a gazetteer of Canadian wild waterways: Mackenzie, Hanbury/Thelon, Back, Kazan, Dubawnt, Harricanaw, Yellowknife/Coppermine, Burnside, Hood, Attawapiskat Winisk, Nahanni, and, of course, the Moisie, to mention only a few. He is a fellow of both the Explorers Club and the Royal Geographical Society based in London, England. Gaskin is a collector of rare books about arctic exploration and lives in Cambridge, Ontario, where he is president of Bradley, Gaskin, and Marshall insurance brokers.

A solo paddler rests in a quiet Missinaibi pool.

CHAPTER THREE

Central Wild

Because James Bay's great rivers are close to large centers of population, many have been dammed for power generation. But long before rivers such as the Mattagami, Abitibi, and La Grande were dammed, they provided an essential link between the fur-rich interior of central Canada and tide-water trading posts on James Bay. Fortunately, rivers such as the Harricanaw, Albany, and Attawapiskat remain much as they were centuries ago, when native paddlers and voyageurs used them to transport goods.

Missinaibi: After the Voyageurs

BY SARA HARRISON

Imagine embarking on a historic river journey that takes you northward from Lake Superior, over a height of land and down the Missinaibi, 265 unimpeded miles to James Bay. It is a sublime and spectacular encounter with a river that has a colorful heritage and an unusual diversity of geologic forms, plants, animals, and bird life. Undiminished in its wilderness character, the Missinaibi remains the only major river in northeastern Ontario that flows freely to James Bay.

It was in anticipation of such a journey that fellow Canadian Outward Bound Wilderness School instructor Louis Barrette and I chose the Michipicoten/Missinaibi route for an instructional canoe trip in the spring of 1981. In late May eight of us gathered on Lake Superior at the mouth of the Michipicoten River: two leaders and six participants from across Canada and as far away as Japan at the beginning of a twenty-eight-day river learning experience. For a day and a half we practiced canoe-rescue techniques, flatwater paddling strokes, and first-aid skills, new friends learning to rely on one another for safety and mutual support.

For Louis and me, instructing a river course was a new experience. We would require a focus different from that of our many personal canoe trips. We would have to help our participants learn to read the river, to assess its dangers, and to maneuver skillfully its ever-changing features. Our goal was to instill a respect for the power of moving water, and to help develop the skills and judgment needed to paddle a remote river safely, thereby enhancing the participants' enjoyment of its challenges. High springtime water levels and cold temperatures would leave little margin for error.

The Michipicoten-Missinaibi-Moose rivers route was once an important fur trade artery connecting James Bay to Lake Superior. From inland posts, furs worth fortunes were carried over portages around many rapids and falls en route to European markets. Through the din of rushing water, you can sometimes hear the ghostly shouts of the fur-brigade paddlers who walked these trails and played these wild waters.

We left behind the cries of herring gulls over Lake Superior and started up the Michipicoten River toward the edge of the Atlantic watershed. Most canoeists opt to drive to the village of Missanabi, avoiding the three hydroelectric power dams along this 62 miles of the historic fur trade route. We wanted to experience the route Indians and voyageurs had traveled; dams or no

dams, covering the whole route was important.

The group adapted quickly to the daily schedules of the trail and began to work out a balance between self-reliance and interdependence. Reaching Dog Lake, headwaters of the Michipicoten, we stopped to pick up a cache of supplies at the village of Missanabi and set out in search of the portage over the height of land between the Atlantic and Hudson Bay watersheds.

Crossing a major height of land was a big event for the voyageurs; yet, we were surprised by how nondescript this portage turned out to be. As we carried our gear along a very ordinary trail, it didn't feel like we were crossing a great divide, but we were thankful not to be portaging around another hydroelectric power dam, and appreciative of the Missinaibi's wilderness character. It is a river valley almost unchanged in appearance since the Ojibwa, Cree, and voyageurs utilized it as a main travel route.

When we finished the short portage, we faced Missinaibi Lake's notorious winds, kicking up ferocious waves. Undaunted, we danced polkas and jigs to stay warm, while we waited for the wind to abate. Back on the water we headed over to Fairy Point, a 115-foot rock face covered with remarkable paintings.

"Missinaibi" is an Ojibwa word that roughly means "pictures on water" or "painted pictograph." It is an apt name, because there are many sites like Fairy Point along the river. No one is certain how old the sites are, exactly who painted the images, or what part they played in native culture. As we looked up at the cliff face from our canoes, the red ocher designs were a delight to the eye, quiet testimony of a way of life now vanished. Images of fish, caribou, and canoes reflected the intimate connection with the earth the native people had once known.

This encounter helped settle us into the rhythms of wilderness travel, its isolation, its silences. No longer were our senses subconsciously filtering information from the world around us; instead they began to soak it all in.

Great Grey Owl—a rare find on the Missinaibi. In recent times, these magnificent birds have been sighted far south of their typical range, passing, on this occasion, through the valley of the Missinaibi.

Slowing down allowed us to see the world with a fresh perspective, less distracted, more attentive to the exquisite detail of the natural beauty all around us.

Much of what pulls me back to the Shield country is this timelessness and deep sense of familiarity. Paddling on a glacier-formed lake and hearing the call of a loon across the water, I felt like I had come home. This, I think, is what I was trying to share with our students.

"Snapper"—beady-eyed denizen of southern Canada. These large freshwater turtles are omnivorous, eating aquatic invertebrates, fish, reptiles, birds, mammals, carrion, vegetation, and the occasional unwary canoeist.

Overleaf: Terraced vegetation types on the shores are evidence of water-level fluctuations on the Missinaibi. When levels are high, rapids are deep and fun, but tent sites must be bushed out because the beaches are flooded.

At the northeast end of Missinaibi Lake we stopped at the site of an old inland trading post. Originally named Missinaibi Lake House, it was the second inland post of the Hudson's Bay Company, built in 1777. Walking around this site, we talked of the rivalry between the North West Company and the Hudson's Bay Company and how, unfortunately, it was oftentimes the Indians who lost out in the fierce competition between the two. It was not hard to imagine brigades of lean, spry men and their bourgeois arriving, exchanging goods, tall tales, new songs, and gossip, and planning careful strategies for trade.

The Missinaibi River has a turbulent start at Quittagene Rapids. They were too high for us to run, so we portaged and took advantage of the swift run-out below to practice upstream ferries, eddy turns, and peel-outs. It was an ideal place to get a feel for the power of the current, and each team strove to combine the right leans with the right strokes.

The next morning, we awoke to a light dusting of snow, a startling—albeit beautiful—reminder that it was still early in the year and the river was fast, and very cold. Not great for dumping.

Our confidence grew as we made our way down the river, lining, shooting, or portaging numerous rapids each day. We took time to allow each canoe team to consider what approach they would take with each rapids. This was a time-consuming, wet, and, at times, frustrating process; but Louis and I felt it was at the heart of learning how to make good river judgments. The hardest part was setting limits when we felt the participants' enthusiasm outmatched their white-water skills.

Missinaibi morning surprise! Author Harrison awakes below Barrel Rapids to find that night-time temperatures have dipped below freezing.

The river flows under the main line of the Canadian Pacific Railway just south of Peterbell Lake and changes from an enclosed watercourse full of rapids, with banks heavily lined with cedar trees, to a river that meanders through a flat, open string bog. One morning, I got up early and savored the crispness of a new spring day on this part of the river. It was a chance for a little uninterrupted journal writing:

> *An early morning mist*
> *lifts off the river*
> *pink salmon clouds*
> *announce the daybreak*

frozen mitts
hang with icy tips
waiting for the start of day.

But the upper Missinaibi leaves little time for reflection: Deadwood Rapids, Split Rock Falls, St. Peter's Portage kept us busy. Getting behind schedule, we opted to portage without scouting rapids for a while. This was quicker, but not nearly as satisfying.

Sometimes, however, we would slow down, tie the canoes together, and have a leisurely lunch rafting down the river, laughing, talking, and letting distance roll by. Other times we would camp early. With thoughts of safety and river running behind us for the day, we would fish and bake, and savor the Shield country, often drifting off to sleep to the sound of rapids rising and falling.

The Trans-Canada Highway crosses the river at the French-speaking community of Mattice, west of Cochrane. That this would be the only place where we would encounter civilization brightened my soul. We quickly replenished our dwindling baking supplies, bought some fresh vegetables, picked up our mail, and continued on. We were glad of the town's hospitality, but it could not compete with the attraction of the river, because the best was yet to come.

A half-day upstream from legendary Thunderhouse Falls, Louis and I decided to ferry across the swiftly moving river and follow a route along the other shore. The others followed in an upstream ferry position, but one of the canoes began dropping closer and closer to the top of the rapid. All we could do was shout, "Paddle harder!" Fortunately they managed to scramble into an eddy. It was a sobering reminder of the river's indifference to poor judgment or lack of skill.

Arrowhead—"Duck Potatoes": This common river plant has edible roots that are full of starch. Indians are said to have opened muskrat houses to get at their caches of this wild food. Canoeists, of course, should opt for the "pick your own" method.

We were lucky. Not so a party traveling ahead of us: two of their group members drowned after going over Thunderhouse Falls.

We heeded signs to pull off the river well above the falls, and to portage through the open pine woods toward the sound of crashing water. At the top of a rise, the anticipation was too much. We dropped our loads and headed out to see what was causing the roar. A hundred feet below us the river pounded with a force that took our breath away.

After exploring the luxurious, moss-covered cliff top, we had lunch on a polished granite shelf by the river, munching in silence while absorbing this stunningly beautiful granite gorge. We were captivated by the awesome power of the river hurtling by us in the glistening sunlight. Knowing we had worked hard to get there made seeing Thunderhouse Falls that much more rewarding—a sweet, good feeling down to our toes.

Below the falls, a solitary stone pillar rises 82 feet out of the boiling river. This is "Conjuring House," a place that held religious significance for the native people of this area. Thinking back to the rock paintings on Missinaibi Lake, we wondered what their beliefs and culture had been like before the arrival of the Europeans.

The most challenging white water on the river lies below the falls. We ran 3 miles of continuous rapids that moved briskly between high, rocky hills speckled with a bright green mosaic of moss and lichen. Emerging into a quiet bay, we were exhilarated and relieved to have paddled this section without mishap.

This was a final test, in a way, for our six students. It was now time for them to rely on their own resources and on what they had learned. From here they would be on their own—four days to Moosonee if all went well. Louis and I would follow about half a day behind them, keeping in touch through notes left at preplanned sites.

Alone, Louis and I took time to savor the river valley. Having left the Canadian Shield at Thunderhouse Falls, we paddled across the James Bay lowlands; we began to see white cliffs of sedimentary rock instead of rough granite outcrops. Gradually the river widened and the surrounding landscape became flatter. We spotted a flock of sandhill cranes. We mused about the progress of the group; but with the current moving us along, sometimes 37 miles a day, we had to be careful not to encroach on their earned independence.

"Conjuring House," a solitary pillar of rock midstream below Thunderhouse Falls, was thought to have had religious significance for the local Indians. For canoeists, this enigmatic butte provides a handy measuring stick for comparing water levels.

We rode the Missinaibi to the place where it joins the Mattagami and becomes the Moose River. Farther down, the Abitibi River makes a dramatic entry, cascading down a series of drops. Near Moosonee, this confluence of rivers spanned nearly 2 miles. Distant sand islands took on a mirage-like quality in moody light. I found myself surprised and intrigued by the changing faces of this portion of the river.

Left: *Beautiful fruits of a bluebead lily, or yellow clintonia, poke through a fern close to the forest floor. These poisonous berries, named after former New York State governor DeWitt Clinton, are part of Missinaibi valley flora.*

Below: *Delicate marsh marigolds reach upward to the Missinaibi sun. This plant is found on river banks and along wet sections of portages. Its leaves are sometimes used as pot herbs but require several short boilings with water changes between.*

In the late afternoon, twenty-eight days after leaving the shores of Lake Superior, Louis and I rendezvoused with our weary but happy group at Bush Island, near Moosonee. Sitting on the beach, we shared our successes, and what we learned from one another and from the river. After a month of river schooling—working, playing, singing, laughing, disagreeing together—we reveled in a good feeling of closeness and camaraderie. Author Sigurd Olson describes this special canoe-country feeling well:

> There would be some things that would never be dimmed by distance or by time, compounded of values that would never be forgotten. The joys and challenges of wilderness, the sense of being part of the country and of an era that was gone. The freedom we had known, silence, timelessness, beauty, companionship, and loyalty and the feeling of fullness and completion that was ours at the end.

Sara Harrison's roots go deep into the wilderness. She has been an instructor and staff trainer at the Voyageur Outward Bound School for six years and an instructor and course director at the Canadian Outward Bound Wilderness School, near Thunder Bay, for four years. Since her 1981 voyage on the Missinaibi, she has led trips on the Misehkow, Albany, Teslin, and Yukon rivers, Other interests include cultural anthropology and dog-sledding. Harrison lives in Minneapolis, Minnesota, where she is an interpreter at the Bell Museum of Natural History.

Although river travel and canoes are synonymous for most of us, there are those who explore riparian worlds by other means in other seasons. A canvas wall tent heated by a portable wood stove, lit by candles inside and moonlight outside, looks appealing even at −22°F.

CHAPTER FOUR

Western Wild

North of the prairies, on the Canadian Shield, there are rivers that have drawn travelers for centuries. Rivers such as the Churchill and Fond du Lac were important to the fur trade. Others, such as the Seal River in northern Manitoba, played a lesser role in the fur trade but attract modern-day voyageurs. The Clearwater rises in northwestern Saskatchewan, flows southeast and then west, eventually entering the Athabasca River at Fort McMurray. Because of its historically important location at the north end of the notorious Methye or La Loche portage, between the Hudson Bay and arctic basins, the Clearwater has been nominated as a Canadian Heritage River.

Clearwater: Gateway to the North

BY BOB HENDERSON

Canoes and wild rivers are synonymous for most people; but the snowshoe also has a place in the recreational re-exploration of Canada's wild rivers. In the tradition of great winter travelers such as Samuel Hearne, William Butler, and the amazing winter packeteers—Canada's first postmen to deliver mail from the Mackenzie to Montreal—I traveled over the height of land from the Churchill River to the Clearwater River and beyond. This journey took six of us over the epic Methye Portage, an important segment of the early Trans-Canada Highway.

The Methye Portage was the most significant obstacle to the regular fur trade. This 12-mile portage to the Clearwater River is the beginning of the northwest—the "Gateway to the North" William Butler called it in 1870. Paddling the Clearwater was the dream of many a trader and explorer because, by crossing the legendary Methye Portage, novice *mangeurs de lard*—pork eaters—became the more prestigious *hommes du nord*.

Making the crossing was as much my dream as it was for any employee of the North West Company. I had crossed the height of land between the Atlantic and Hudson Bay watersheds many times on canoe routes west of Grand Portage, but only the Clearwater could make the past live again.

Since the Clearwater, I have felt a magical affinity with history and with the land. I now have a sense of cultural fit, as if I was embraced and strengthened by the connections made during that winter on the Clearwater.

Our group was united by a desire for an extended winter trip in a historical context. More practically, as students of the University of Alberta's Exploration Program within the Department of Physical Education, we had field credits to earn. My role as a graduate student was to oversee this winter adventure with an interdisciplinary focus. We selected the La Loche/Clearwater route because of its historic importance.

At White Mud Falls on the Clearwater River, author Bob Henderson marveled at the way ice and water were intertwined in what he saw as "playful give and take." This Canadian Heritage River is also a favorite of white-water paddlers in summer.

While there were many individual educational objectives for this enterprise, historical retracing was the common denominator. We knew the river had been a favored winter home for native people due to its abundant wildlife and good

Far left, "Hot camping" in the traditions of Canada's native people involves making a frame of wooden poles that will support the tent and fly. A stout 20-foot ridge pole also supports the stove pipe; Left, When the wind shifts and blocks the stove pipe, causing smoke to fill the tent, a flap of wood split from a large log can be wired to a long stick to deflect the wind; Below left, Indian legend says that toboggans should be stored with their running surfaces away from the south so as not to offend the south wind, which could create unwelcome slush.

hunting. It was a critical link in the fur trade transportation network, and it was used as a corridor to the Arctic by many of the great explorers. During the trip, pathfinders such as George Back, Franklin, and Butler would grow to be more than just historic names. My quest within this vibrant, historical context was described by William C. James: "exploration of the wilderness [is] a voyage into the interior of the self."

We headed north from La Loche town site on a January morning. We felt much as George Back did when he described setting out at the same place 150 years earlier. Back's journal might have been ours:

> There is something exciting in the first start even upon an ordinary journey. The bustle of preparation—the act of departing, which seems like a decided step taken—the prospect of change, and consequent stretching out of the imagination—have at all times the effect of stirring the blood. ... Before me were novelty and enterprise; hope, curiosity and the love of adventure were my companions.

We covered the first 10 miles of the historic Methye Portage in strained, uphill steps. Then, suddenly, against a completely horizontal perspective, we came to the edge of the Clearwater valley. The vertical drop was only 558 feet, but in contrast to the strikingly flat land, it looked much higher. For Franklin, this was one of the "most picturesque" scenes in the northern part of America:

> We arrived at the summit of a lofty chain of mountains commanding the most picturesque and romantic prospect we had yet seen in this country. Two ranges of high hills ran parallel to each other for several miles until the faint blue haze hides their particular characteristics. The distant prospect is surpassed only in grandeur by the wild scenery that appears immediately below our feet. ... At one spot, termed the Cockscomb, the passenger stands insulated as it were on a small slip, where a false step might precipitate him into the glen. From this place Mr. Back took an interesting and accurate sketch of the view.

William Butler was inspired in 1870 not by the beauty of the spot but with the realization that he stood on the edge of immense watersheds and travelways:

> This long portage ... is not a bad position from whence to take a bird's eye view of the Great North ... the only slope is to the North; from here to the frozen sea, 1,000 miles as wild swans fly, is one long, gradual descent.

Clearwater: Gateway to the North 55

Being there, reading this material, searching for the Cockscomb and the site where Back drew his sketch, we were struck by what he called "the genius of the place."

The stillness of winter seemed to originate in the valley. It was as if winter slowly gained momentum as it followed the gradual north slope of the arctic basin. Our pace slowed to about 10 miles per day, and we enjoyed a rest day relaxing in this valley filled with the genius of benign winter.

We winced at Franklin's much more ambitious 16-miles-per-day pace, but we reveled in the opportunity to have a good look around. The Clearwater was known as a haven for wildlife, including deer, moose, wolf, and bear; but, although I observed winter-kill drama etched in fresh animal tracks, and there were animal signs everywhere, we saw precious little wildlife.

The Methye Portage enters about midway along the length of the Clearwater. In winter, this point in the valley is a meandering white highway, perfect for snowshoeing but not much of a river for white-water enthusiasts. Upstream, though, there are many wild-water stretches that draw enthusiastic paddlers in warm weather. And downstream the river is far from spent.

This rediscovering of history warmed my spirits. I found a rhythm and lyrical meaning in slow-paced snowshoeing. Each day offered long periods of silent travel, favorite times in which I seemed to melt in the winter landscape. Unloading toboggans, cutting poles, sawing and splitting firewood linked us closely to the land. Of course, we had our down sleeping bags and other twentieth-century trappings, but more than ever before I had thrown off that other world: our footwear was moosehide moccasins, our clothing was wool; our food was traditional, not freeze-dried or prepackaged; and most of our equipment was wood and canvas.

In the Clearwater River region the white-tailed deer is at the northern extent of its range. Although up to five million of these animals are shot by hunters or killed by dogs or car collisions each year in North America, multiple litters and early reproductive age allow this deer to be one of the most abundant large-game animals.

A strange freedom surfaced in this primitive setting, in activity, materials, and desire linked so closely with the land. Traditional style has this reward, but, in its reliance on large amounts of wood for fuel and tent poles, it has a significant impact on the land. Fortunately, winter camps rarely correspond with those used in summer—summer sites are open and exposed, while winter sites must be sheltered, not right on a waterway—so we were not camping

Left: *Following the tradition of explorers and the winter packeteers, who carried mail between fur trade posts, an expedition member uses a 20-foot tumpline to haul a loaded toboggan.*

in heavily used locations.

The meandering Clearwater drops 98 feet over Whitemud Falls just beyond the Alberta border. Openings in the ice shrouded in thick mist revealed winter's constant struggle to contain the energy in the falls. Here we took the portage trail, leaving the river for the first time. Uphill hauling in deep snow made us all appreciate the wind-packed snow on the river. With 12 miles of intermittent rapids below the falls, we had to read the ice carefully for weak spots.

Downstream, at a limestone gorge, we stopped for a bite. With jaws stiffened by the –4°F temperatures, I read from Franklin's 1820 journal:

> *We afterwards followed the river as far as the Pine Portage, when we passed through a very romantic defile of rocks which presented the appearance of Gothic ruins, and their rude characters were happily contrasted with the softness of the snow, and the darker foliage of the pines which crowned their summits.*

The splintered dolomite pillars before us had to be Franklin's Gothic ruins! Here was a landscape apparently unchanged in more than 150 years; it was as if Franklin had passed through just yesterday. It's sad, but such sites need to be protected to preserve their authenticity. While most of the Saskatchewan portion of the Clearwater is protected by the Canadian Heritage River designation, this Alberta part of the lower river is not.

The earliest trade route between eastward- and northward-flowing waters followed the Methye Portage and the Clearwater River. The route was discovered by Peter Pond in 1778 and used for more than a century by fur traders and explorers, including Alexander Mackenzie, John Franklin, William Butler, and George Simpson.

The Clearwater, like many northern rivers, has not escaped exploitation for economic gain. In the late 1960s, it was decided that the river's hydro-power yield was inadequate for development—for the moment—but logging activity downstream was in full swing and would soon shatter our link with the past.

On day 13 our trip was complete. We walked into town, hauling our toboggans along the paved sidewalk to the bus station. But it was more a start than a finish.

As novelist Peter Such wrote:

> *We all need a sense of our past, and how our present and indeed our future grow out, to see ourselves as part of that continuing tradition as it keeps evolving and not separate from it.*

Waxing runners using a candle and a heated ax head stops icing and makes heavy loads easier to haul.

To this Grey Owl can add:

> *Each succeeding generation takes on the works by those who pass along leaving behind*
> *them a tradition and a standard of achievement, that must be lived up to by those who*
> *would claim a membership in the Brotherhood of the Keepers of the Trail.*

This winter trek on the Clearwater showed me that there really is a "Brotherhood of the Keepers of the Trail"; indeed, we all need a sense of the past to evolve wisely as culture and wilderness clash on so many fronts. Perhaps it is as Keepers of the Trail we can build a culture better adapted to our needs in nature and the needs of such wild places. The Clearwater was my beginning. For the first time I saw the land and its heritage not from the outside looking in, but as part of the inside.

Bob Henderson canoed his way through Lakefield College School and McMaster University before joining the University of Alberta Master's program, which took him down the Clearwater in the winter of 1980. From 1973 to 1980, he was a summer canoe-tripping guide at Camp Ahmek in Ontario's Algonquin Provincial Park. Since then he has rediscovered historical routes from Tasmania to Baffin Island. Henderson lives in Dundas, Ontario, where he is a lecturer in Outdoor Education at McMaster University.

Lynx: Studies have shown that this resident of the Clearwater valley is actually more efficient at hunting rabbits and hares in winter than in any other season. Wide furry paws act as snowshoes; the lynx's long legs move with ease through deep snow and its muted colors blend into a winter forest's gloom. What looks like a bushy tail in this photograph is actually the well-insulated inside of an outstretched back leg.

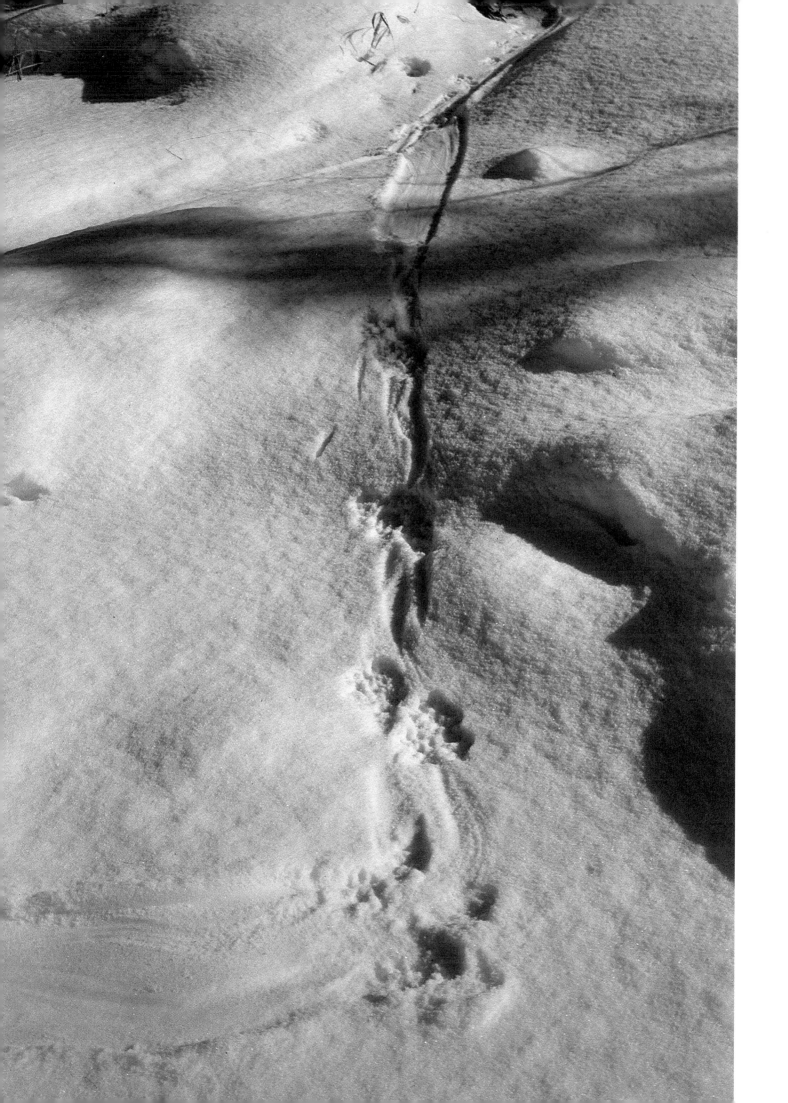

Opposite: *Playful in winter, too, the river otter saves time and energy by folding its front legs back and sliding along on the snow. Even going up hill, this animal manages to get in a few slips between steps.*

A Swainson's hawk crouches over winter kill.

River meets sky in the land of the midnight sun.

CHAPTER FIVE

Arctic Wild

Remote and unpopulated, the rivers of Arctic North America are a throwback to a prehistoric time, when there was nothing but landscape to celebrate the great forces of nature. In Alaska, many rivers still swell from the melt waters of remnants of the great glaciers that quietly continue to shape the mountainous Northwest. On the north slope, the Colville flows up to the Beaufort Sea and the Noatak flows west to the Chukchi Sea. Farther down, the Kuskokwim flows south and west to the Bering Sea, and the Susitna flows out to the Gulf of Alaska. Wild, icy cold, unfettered. But the grandparent of all Arctic rivers has to be the Yukon, rising on the border of the Yukon Territory and British Columbia, and arcing westward through Alaska, draining the Porcupine, Tanana and Koyukuk, until it too reaches tidewater at Norton Sound.

Yu-kan-ah: The Great River

BY KATHLEEN USHER

Leaving the village of Tanana, Alaska, anxious to get back on the Yukon river after a bewildering four-day funeral potlatch for a village elder, I realized that, like our Athapaskan hosts, we had become part of the river. We had lived on her banks, paddled her strong brown waters, and renewed our bodies with the red flesh of her salmon. We had been frightened and enchanted by her many moods. We had accepted the river as Life.

I had come north with a friend, Monique Dykstra, to experience the place and its people firsthand with a three-month adventure that—with luck—would take us from Whitehorse, capital of the Yukon, to the Bering Sea along nearly the full 1,979-mile extent of North America's fifth-longest river to arctic tidewater on the Bering Sea—the watercourse the Indians call "Yu-kan-ah," meaning "great river." On June 15, 1993, we eased our laden canoe into the imposing 5-mile-per-hour current and whizzed past the city of Whitehorse. It felt like giving birth: months of preparation, one final push, and we were out, just the two of us and our gear in a wonderfully seaworthy 18-foot Nahanni canoe newly baptized *My Heart*. All those days of agonizing over what to bring, setting up three food drops, and calling airlines were gone. We were on the river.

Sweeping north from where it rises at Tagish Lake on the Yukon/British Columbia border, then west, through Alaska, to the Bering Sea, the Yukon is a river of many faces. Outside Whitehorse, steep sandy banks are home to swallows that swoop down over the river, then up, drawing our eyes to imposing *hodads*, or natural sand gargoyles, perched in a line atop the banks. There are bald eagles on almost every tree branch, juveniles mostly, looking awkward with their spotty breasts and small heads. A black bear sliding down the sandy bank, paws splayed, back

From the Gold Rushers of '98 to this young German in '93, the Yukon captures the imagination of adventurous spirits. He built this raft by hand and floated it the length of the river over three summers.

between front, to drink from the great river, brought us back to reality and to the idea of sharing this magnificent valley with its many other living creatures.

Toward Dawson City, site of the Klondike gold rush of 1897, the river narrows between rocky rounded hillsides overlooked by snow-dusted mountains in the background. From this point on, silt from glacier-fed tributaries gives the river the look of coffee with cream. At the village of Eagle, the river enters Alaska, and then past Circle, to open onto the Yukon Flats, a sprawling wetland with

Clear morning skies world billow, toward mid-day, with thunderheads that looked like huge genies rising from their atmospheric lanterns.

40,000 lakes, and 25,000 miles of streams and oxbows, that nurtures the lives of moose, bears, beavers, two million waterfowl, and occasional people of both aboriginal and European descent. And eventually, the great river arcs south, finally sweeping up north again to meet the sea at Norton Sound.

At these latitudes, in the land of the midnight sun, the logic of day and night just didn't make sense, so we changed our paddling routine. Rather than bake in the midday sun, we began setting off at six in the evening, when the sun was still high but the heat less intense. We would paddle until about three in the morning and then camp again. During that time, the sky would change from a noontime blue to evening pink, before darkening to indigo as we slept. We saw no stars for two months!

On our seasonally adjusted paddling schedule, we often arrived at fish camps in the wee hours of the morning, worried that the sled dogs, tied on stakes by the river, would awaken everyone with howls and barks. No sooner would dogs settle than children would come down the bank to see who had arrived. Five- and six-year-olds would be up at 3:00 A.M., playing ball, laughing and running about. Women would be hanging laundry on the line.

Sometimes, though, we would land at curious unpeopled constellations of frame houses. At the first of these, it was the brightly colored roofs on the bank that caught my eye as we drifted along. We tethered *My Heart* to some scrub and clambered up the bank. Against a stand of shimmering green aspen was a miniature village, each hobbit-sized house of red and blue surrounded by freshly painted white picket fences. We learned that when a member of a village dies, he or she is buried and a small house built in which the spirit can continue to exist. Objects important to the deceased are placed inside. We were also taught that these spirit yards are always situated upriver from the village to allow the wisdom of the dead to continue to flow past the living.

Throughout July, we were blessed with unbelievably fine weather and welcome from everyone along the way. People we met generously feasted us on delicious smoked-salmon strips, highbush-cranberry jelly, garden lettuce, cucumbers, and the odd moose or caribou steak, before setting us back on the river. As the days ticked by, we crossed into Alaska, at the village of Eagle, and then past the village of Circle, onto the broad expanses of Yukon Flats. Clear morning skies would billow, toward midday, with thunderheads that looked like huge genies rising from their atmospheric lanterns. Come evening, the clouds would dissipate and we would rise again to blue sky. But all was about to change.

A husky reclines on a truck in Mountain Village, Alaska.

Cutting up seal meat with "ulu" knife in Russian Mission.

Opposite: *Kids playing in our canoe My Heart in Marshall, Alaska. Working dogs are tied to stakes in the background.*

In early August, surrounded by these genies, we came to an unexpected fork in the river. Sticks we threw into the water seemed to drift, then circle, as if they too were stymied by the confusing currents. Eventually, we chose the wider channel and resumed paddling with a typical midafternoon breeze at our backs. Suddenly, the channel veered ninety degrees, and we turned to meet a stiff, warm wind that hit our faces like a slap. In no time, the silty brown waters churned, and whitecaps slapped over the gunwales.

A quick glance at the shore told us we were losing ground to the blow. With sign language and shouts, we agreed to pull over to a tiny scrub-covered sandbar. As I stepped out of the boat to pull us in, something stung my face, then my leg. Then small holes started appearing on the orange tarp that covered *My Heart*'s load amidships. Embers? Fire!

Across the channel, 100- to 230-foot flames were devouring the spruce. With embers flying and dust and smoke obscuring our vision, we tied the boat to our waists and dragged it to temporary shelter on the sandbar. Trapped together beside *My Heart* we fixed coffee and drank it laced with precious Irish whiskey to contemplate our future. I thought of Homer's warring gods, each demonstrating his might in a supernatural battle of fire against water. Finally, around midnight, the wind began to settle. Smoke mushroomed up against the dusty pink sky and finally dissipated into thin plumes of gray.

Even after this close call with the fire, I became aware of a most comforting sense of familiarity, of home, on the river. Whenever we spent more than a day or two in one spot, either because of weather or to spend time with people, getting back on the water, the sound of the silt hissing against the hull felt like coming home. Time on the river gave me the head-space to absorb the stories of the people we met along the way. Their faces and voices blended with the river in a rush of water as relentless as time slipping through the cracks of a native culture now on the cusp of either dying out or resurrecting. When we stopped for the four-day potlatch and all of those new sensations, even this experience was gently contextualized by the hours in the canoe, drifting, thinking, floating our way toward the sea.

Like the salmon battling against the current, many of the white people we met who called the Yukon their home had found it impossible to "go with the flow" in the places where they'd been brought up. The contrast between white and native river inhabitants was at times jarring. White folk, by and large, were escaping the community and rejecting the culture into which they were born,

Steep, sandy banks shoot up from the river near its headwaters and are crowned with hodads *perched like gargoyles reaching skyward.*

while First Nations people fought to hold onto the remnants of theirs.

Every person to whom we spoke equated the river with life; their food, their transportation, and their history flowed in and along the water. And yet, without exception, the river had taken the life of a loved one, sometimes even wiping out entire families. Outboards or snowmobiles usually figured in the deaths, but there were many unsolved mysteries of boats lost, bodies never found. On calm, misty mornings I would sometimes stand on the shore with my coffee, remember our close call with the wind-driven fire, and wonder what lay ahead for Monique and me.

We had not long to wait. About the 600-mile mark of our journey, we were drifting effortlessly along the bank with the current—a "float break." Our guard was down. Suddenly Monique yelled "Sweeper!" as we broad-sided a huge fallen cottonwood tree sticking out into the channel. Into the water we went. The force of the current and the shock of sudden immersion snatched my breath. We scrambled to hang on, arms slung over the exposed hull as other underwater logs and sweepers bashed our legs and threatened to pull us down. It was all we could do to pull the boat to a stop by grasping tufts of horsetail grass on the shore. Fortunately, we escaped this, our one and only capsize, unscathed, except for an easily repaired crack in the side of *My Heart*, one paddle, one yellow shirt, two thermal coffee mugs, and a healthy dose of pride lost to the mighty Yuke. It was an important wake-up call to our vulnerability

The weather turned abruptly in the first days of August. The silent stillness of summer mornings punctuated by birdsong were replaced by wind flapping against nylon and cottonwoods rustling ominously overhead. Paddling became arduous and slow-going as the wind stirred up boat-spinning waves on the widening expanses of the river. We slowed to about 25 miles per day from our usual rate of about 40 to 50 miles every twelve hours. Unsettling though it was to contemplate, I began to wonder if we would make it all the way to the sea. I began to regret the leisurely pace and lingering encounters with river dwellers we'd enjoyed upriver. Driven by the need to finish, my arms ached with each stroke into what, at times, felt like frothy wet, brown cement.

By mid-August the treed hillsides were showing bursts of orange, and a golden hue had replaced the deep green of the cottonwoods. The Kowitchan wool toque I had stashed at the bottom of my pack became indispensable at night and stayed on my head longer and longer each morning. We learned that, with fall winds on the Yukon, the heavens open and rains begin in abundance.

Right: *Good-bye Yukon River. The view from the Alaskan Airlines jet out of St. Mary's heading toward Anchorage. The Yukon delta stretches out over 200 miles.*

Below: *Author in canoe near Carmacks, Yukon Territory.*

Joe Creek Village (abandoned) on Lake Laberge, Y.T., with wild roses blooming in foreground.

Apart from three gloriously clear days, it rained every day in the last four weeks of our journey, sometimes for a couple of hours, more often all day long.

We got increasingly nervous about finishing the trip. "When freeze-up comes," said one woman, who had taken pity on us by inviting us in for cinnamon buns and coffee (and a dry place to sleep), "every morning you get up and you look, and you hold your thumb like this to the window—'Yup, it's still moving.' And then on the day you think it's going to stop, you check it every half-hour and pretty soon it just stops." The last thing we wanted was to get stranded in ice, even if there were kindred spirits along the way to help us out.

Between Holy Cross and Russian Mission, we crossed from Athapascan Indian territory to that of the coastal Yu'pik Inuit. The river signaled this transition by widening out again, as it did at Yukon Flats. With mountains on three sides and a sweeping expanse of river glinting in the fall sunset, a sandbar seemed the perfect place to stop for a quick rest before moving on.

As we started setting up the tent, two young men in camouflage shirts and ear protectors pulled up in the largest fishing boat I'd seen yet on the river. Against the winds and waves, it looked much more seaworthy than our old friend *My Heart*. Marshall and Willie introduced themselves and explained that they'd just gotten a moose on a nearby island and thought they might come by to share it with the "floaters" (a term used up and down the river for people paddling the Yukon). As we ate fried moose heart and steak, they told us about their life on the coast and how it is a Yu'pik custom for coastal people to bring gifts from the sea to the people upriver.

Two days later, still well upriver from the sea, we were in the house of Sandra Kozevnikoff, a Yu'pik language trainer in Russian Mission. In the tradition described to us by Marshall and Willie, a fellow came in and dumped a dead seal on Sandra's wooden kitchen floor. Sandra explained that, at one time, seals followed the salmon upriver, and that in the past her people were in the habit of hunting and eating them. But now, seals were scarce, almost never seen. It was only when someone from the coast, coming upriver to hunt moose with gifts of meat from the sea, that people in Russian Mission got to enjoy seal meat. It was my privilege to help Sandra cut up the seal blubber into bite-size squares with traditional curved *ulu* knives, and to watch as everyone in the village streamed through her house, Sandra offering with pride a taste of seal, food that was once a staple in their lives.

We had to move. By mid-September winter was definitely in the air.

Dustings of snow came and went, and the wind continued to overpower us at times, broadsiding the canoe to the waves, sending icy water crashing over the gunwales. People we met in Pilot Station, a small village 75 miles from the sea, made it clear that they thought we were out of our minds to be carrying on this late in the season. Still, we clung to the original plan. We remained hell-bent to finish the trip.

After we left Pilot Station, the headwind wound its way into a gale. In the bow, I bobbed before a vast expanse of rolling whitecaps, spindrift stinging my face. The opposite shore had disappeared in the storm. Uncertainty ached in the pit of my stomach. A harrowing hour of paddling got us almost nowhere. To carry on would risk getting killed. We beached the canoe, scrambled up the cutbank, and crawled onto a grassy knoll beside a mountain that separated us from the village.

The solace of clouds floating in a northern sky, the hiss of silt under the boat, the river felt like home.

We thrashed with the prospect of abandoning our journey, 2 miles out of Pilot Station, 70 miles from the sea, 1,864 miles of river under *My Heart*'s keel. These figures, however, evaporated into meaninglessness as we reached to accept the inevitable end of our journey. The birds were gone, the moose were venturing onto higher ground, the salmon had completed their lunge up the river, the bears had gorged themselves and were bunkering down for winter.

It was time for the two of us, two women from Montreal in a white canoe, to accept that the river which had so gallantly escorted us this far was no longer in the mood for visitors. Difficult as it was, we had learned by now to accept her moods and rhythms. Here, the people belong to the land, and the land is ruled by the river. She would have her way. She rules this country, and her children must obey. The lessons we'd learned would not soon be forgotten.

Kathleen Usher began canoeing with day outings into the Quebec Laurentians that led to extended summer trips in remote LaVerendrye Provincial Park. These experiences took her into environmental biology at McGill University in Montreal, and later to study outdoor and experiential education at Queen's University in Kingston, Ontario. Prior to this Yukon River trip in 1993, Kathleen was a naturalist with the Canadian Parks Service. Since then, Kathleen gave birth to daughter Emilie-Anne in 1995, and continues interpretive work as an environmental education consultant with A-D Naturalists in Montreal.

Arctic reflections: Author Mason's companions set out across calm and open headwaters of the Hood River. Favorable winds have kept pack ice pinned against the opposite shore, leaving a wide lead for making headway toward the river.

CHAPTER SIX

Barren Land Wild

Above the Arctic Circle in the central Northwest Territories is the region where Sir John Franklin and his men made their epic explorations in the early 1800s. Franklin's party left Fort Enterprise, near Great Slave Lake, and traveled north via the Coppermine River. Paddling bark canoes, they mapped the coast of the Arctic Ocean east of the Coppermine and eventually struggled south again up a river named for Franklin's steadfast midshipman, Robert Hood. Modern-day canoeists usually follow Franklin down the Coppermine River; a smaller number have sought kinship with Franklin in the valleys of the Hood, Burnside, and Mara rivers. These are remote rivers with ice-cold wild water and compelling historical intrigue.

Hood: In Franklin's Wake

BY BILL MASON

I awoke to the sound of steadily pounding arctic rain, which, I sensed, would continue for days. It's strange how you can tell. My five companions—Wally Schaber, Bruce Cockburn, Gilles Lebreque, Alan Whatmough, and Gilles Couet—were still asleep, or pretending to be. I rolled over in the luxurious warmth of my bag and reveled in the feeling of remoteness and unlimited distance that brought us here.

For the first time since our Hood River trip began, we didn't have to break camp. We had two days in our schedule to enjoy the spectacular scenery around Wilberforce Falls, rain or no. The day before we had all agreed, despite overcast light, that this 164-foot falls and 2.5-mile canyon was the most spectacular sight we had ever seen, better even than Virginia Falls on the Nahanni River.

Until the summer of 1983, my favorite canoe trip was a toss-up between two Lake Superior rivers: the Pukaskwa, and the Dog River with spectacular Denison Falls. I still favor those trips for pure enjoyment, but the Hood pumped adrenalin through my veins at record rates.

The Hood flows from west to east for several hundred miles through the central Northwest Territories, paralleling the arctic coastline about 100 miles inland from the Arctic Ocean. Just before Bathurst Inlet, the river does a right-angle turn and crashes north over Wilberforce Falls into Arctic Sound.

We were concerned that even in July the lakes would still be locked in ice. We dreaded the possibility of being ice-bound; we badly wanted to spend our only two days to spare at Wilberforce Falls. We had heard stories of people being stuck for weeks and having to haul laden canoes over ice floes.

A seldom-seen treasure of the Hood River is a second channel at Wilberforce Falls that runs only when water is high. In the red quartzite rock, a lucky traveler can find small deposits of semi-precious amethyst.

We were very fortunate. Our Yellowknife-based pilot was able to land in the headwaters of the river; while we were on these lakes, a steady northwest wind kept chunks of ice pinned against the south shore, leaving a narrow lead along the north shore. Occasionally we had to make a short haul over ice when the lead closed, but compared to the trip reports we'd read, our entry to the Hood was smooth.

There are two basic kinds of terrain through which the river flows. There is difficult walking terrain—grassy hummocks sitting in icy water, not quite strong enough to support a person's weight. Hummocks make for cold, wet feet and

sore ankles. The other terrain is a delight to walk on—meandering ridges of sand and gravel, called "eskers," that snake for great distances over the treeless landscape. These mark the location of rivers that flowed beneath the last great ice sheets.

The wet terrain was home to healthy populations of mosquitoes. When the weather was cold, warm clothing protected us, but still our faces, hands, and necks were exposed. Strong winds gave relief from the bugs, but occasionally they were intolerable. Most times, though, the scenery, the river, the rapids, the caribou, the musk-ox, the food, and the fun made the mosquitoes easier to take.

My greatest delight was to finish supper early and set out on long hikes. From most eskers I could see several days' journey in all directions. Sometimes I could almost see Sir John Franklin and his men trekking toward the south in August 1821, carrying their one battered canoe, trying to follow the eskers back to Fort Enterprise after an epic summer of discovery. What might it have been that drove them to leave their homes in England to explore this barren, hostile, and cruel landscape? I also thought of how these explorers chose not to adopt the ways of the native people, who made this forbidding land home by following the migrating herds of caribou.

I thought of Franklin's desperate plight. They were out of food, and winter had come early; for more than half of them it was a death march. Midshipman Hood fell behind. When one of the guides showed up with fresh meat, Franklin became suspicious: it was Hood. The guide had shot him; and he, in turn, had to be executed. Just the thought of these events sent shivers up my spine.

Barren-ground caribou step lightly away from approaching canoeists. Like all four subspecies of caribou that live in the Northwest Territories, both male and female barren-ground caribou have antlers that are shed and regrown every year. These animals are members of the Bathurst Herd (approximately 180,000 strong) that winters below the tree line north of Great Slave Lake and calves, after a long annual migration, on the east side of Bathurst Inlet.

The region is described as "barren," yet we saw more wildlife in one trip than I've seen in a lifetime of southern canoeing. The diversity of living creatures may be low, but the numbers are staggering. It's difficult to describe the thrill of paddling by thousands of caribou. The caribou were traveling along the north shore of the Hood toward the west. We were traveling east and it took two days to paddle by the herd. We were amazed that such terrain could support these vast herds. The secret of their success is migration, an amazing mechanism that prevents them from overbrowsing.

Encountering musk-ox was another highlight of the trip. We saw many indi-

Although wolves north of the tree line are informally called "tundra wolves," to differentiate them from the timber wolf that lives below the tree line and the arctic wolf that lives on the arctic islands, all these dog-like carnivores belong to the same genus and species, *Canis lupus*. For tundra wolves the most important prey animal is caribou.

Left: *With no trees in the arctic, birds must nest on the ground, which requires good camouflage coloring. These semi-palmated plover eggs blend in nicely. They are also purposely oriented with small ends toward the center of the nest. Some scientists think that this four-egg pattern makes the clutch easier for the adults to incubate; others postulate that the pattern is a heat-saving adaptation that reduces airflow over the eggs when the nest is unattended.*

Below: *From high land above this campsite on the Hood, it is possible to see several days' journey in all directions.*

Left: *River beauty—a showy far-northern relative of fireweed that grows on gravelly river banks across the arctic.*

Below: *A scenic and historic river named by explorer Sir John Franklin after his midshipman Robert Hood. Almost dead from a diet of shoe leather and lichen, Hood was shot and killed on October 20, 1821, by his tent-mate Michel Terohaute, an Iroquois Indian.*

The brink of Wilberforce Falls:
two falls totalling more than
200 feet are thought to be the
highest falls in the world north
of the Arctic Circle. Here, there
are no barriers to stop curious
onlookers from falling over
the edge.

viduals, as well as groups of two, three, and four. The largest groups were nine and ten and usually had calves among them.

We had it on authority that musk-ox rarely charge; they are much more likely to run away. On one occasion we saw two musk-ox in a clump of willows. Alan, Bruce, Gilles, and I went up onto a ridge where they could see us. Wally and Gilles Couet sneaked through the 3-foot-high willows to get a picture of them. The musk-ox turned to look in the direction of their approach. Wally and Gilles were not going unnoticed, but there was no way to tell them! With cameras ready, Wally and Gilles peeked around from behind the willows. There, staring right back at them barely 10 yards away, were two confused musk-ox! All of a sudden they butted their heads together and turned to look back at Wally and Gilles. Wally made a swath through the willows back to the canoes; Gilles widened it. We never did convince Wally and Gilles that head-butting is anything but a preliminary act to all-out charge.

Although we never saw a wolf, we saw many wolf scats and footprints. For me, the presence of wolves is a sign that all is well and in a natural state. We were also privileged to catch a glimpse of a peregrine falcon. Whenever I see one I am touched with sadness that they are so rare.

The rapids were runnable, Class I to Class III. There were a few that we chose to line because of the frigid water and air temperatures. Moreover, losing a canoe or having an injury would turn an enjoyable trip into a nightmare. It was with great reluctance and disappointment that we lined our first rapid, but our disappointment was short-lived; almost everything else that wasn't classified as a falls proved to be runnable.

We were approaching a set described in our trip notes as "absolutely unrunnable." We pulled over to the left shore in preparation for a landing. But no, not yet! Ahead was a huge boulder jutting out into the current. You could see calm water just beyond the rock. The two Gilleses drifted their canoe right by the rock and back-paddled into the eddy. It wasn't that difficult but there was no room for error; the eddy was just above the brink of a wild rapid.

Long portages across tundra inspire novel transportation solutions. These portagers are using what is affectionately known as the "Jimmy Hoffa Method."

We set up for the back ferry and followed suit. We drifted by the rock, and a couple of hefty backstrokes put us in the eddy. I looked back for Alan and Bruce and was horrified to see that the current had grabbed their canoe and swung it right out into center stream. They had no choice but to attempt a run!

Right: *Mason's compadres settle in for a feed of fresh lake trout.*

Gilles Lebreque taking a solo run through a difficult stretch of rapids.

Wally, the two Gilleses, and I wouldn't have bet a nickel on their chances of getting through upright or in one piece, even with their spray cover. We would have to get there quickly to rescue them from the ice-cold water. Yet we couldn't move; we were horror-struck. They plummeted down into the maelstrom of plunging waves and almost disappeared. Slowly the canoe surfaced with water pouring off the decks like a submarine. They were still upright! They disappeared and reappeared once more—still upright. They emerged at the bottom still floating, but just. We were ecstatic, laughing and shouting as we leaped into our canoes for a sneak run tight to the shore, anxious to get to them before they sank.

They had shot something as extreme as anything I've ever seen; they hit it dead center where the rocks were all buried. They had kept their balance and powered through—no fancy maneuvers—but we still believed they might sink before reaching shore. As we rounded the bend, there was Alan reclining on a pack on shore, smoking his pipe. Bruce was wringing out some clothes. Alan said with utter disdain, "I see you took the easy route." We all cracked up! The two least-experienced canoeists had run a rapid that looked more like a falls.

There was one other stretch of rapids that we debated about running, a long gorge with several small waterfalls. In bright sunshine the rapids looked turbulent but inviting. We decided to portage all the gear to the end and run the rapids empty after lunch. As we ate a leisurely lunch on a high knoll overlooking the gorge, the sunlight gave way to gray cloud. My enthusiasm for running the turbulent rapid waned with the dropping temperature. I was relieved when Wally asked, "How badly do you want to run that?" I looked up at the gray sky and said, "Not very." We decided to portage, but how we hated to waste a good run.

When we looked back up the rapid there was Gilles Lebreque taking one last look. He decided to try it solo. We grabbed our cameras and recorded Gilles making every move exactly as planned. I looked again at the cold bleak sky and decided that I wasn't heartbroken that we hadn't tried. I only wished Gilles hadn't made it look so easy.

As enthusiastic as we were about running rapids, we were never disappointed when the sound of distant white water turned out to be a thundering waterfall. I can sit for days watching them and I love to clamber over rocks and view, photograph, and sketch them from every conceivable angle. Most of the waterfalls on the Hood were preceded or followed by a gorge. Because of the absence of trees it was very easy to view them from any angle, but it wasn't until one of us stood beside the falls that we got any sense of scale.

Apart from the scenery, it was the light that set the mood. The sun hardly dipped below the horizon so we enjoyed more than four hours of warm twilight glow. The cold austere landscape took on the warm color of the sky. Bleak rock faces shone like gold. Often the wind dropped at night to a gentle whisper. It was a time of magic.

The fact that you can see for miles and miles in all directions makes the land feel limitless, yet it is so fragile. It could never sustain or absorb great numbers of people. It has always amazed me that the native people, though here for thousands of years, somehow kept their numbers more or less constant in relation to their source of food. Yet our well-being depends on increased growth in the economy and population. The end result can only be overcrowding and depletion of resources, all at the expense of the environment and the other creatures that share the earth with us.

On the Hood, we were the only human beings within hundreds of miles, yet we were deeply aware of the impact that just six of us had on the land. Camped at Wilberforce Falls before our final run to the sea, it was an effort to find enough wood just to heat a pail of soup or a pot of tea. We also cooked with a gas stove, but we really enjoyed the small fire. Yet we all realized how quickly the shore could be denuded of firewood.

Prior to Mason's Hood River trip, Wilberforce Canyon had never been paddled. Somehow (the crew won't say) they got into a large eddy below the falls. This picture documents the start of a first attempt at shooting the canyon.

The sheer size of the land and its remoteness from our world have kept it relatively unchanged; but what was once a journey of one or two years just to get here from the south can now be accomplished in two days from Ottawa. Now it's only the cost of getting here that protects the land from overuse. With the high cost, ice-coated lakes, mosquitoes, and black-flies, I doubt that the land will ever be overrun with sightseers. Still, it is difficult to look on this land and its varied life and not care about what happens to it.

Bill Mason was a man of many talents who captured North American hearts with films and books that shared his love for the canoe and sensitivity to the wilderness. As a filmmaker, he was best known for his Path of the Paddle *series. He won fifty-eight national and international awards, including two British Academy Awards and two Oscar nominations. After the release of his last film,* Waterwalker, *Mason retired from the National Film Board and turned his full attention to writing and painting. Mason died in 1988.*

A brilliant sunset turns the waters of the Bonnet Plume burnt orange behind the silhouette of canoe and paddle.

Mountain Wild

There are many wild rivers in the Yukon that rise high in the Rockies. Some make their way to the Pacific as tributaries of the Yukon River, others to the Beaufort Sea as tributaries of the Mackenzie. But on the north slope of the continent are rivers such as the Blackstone, Ogilvie, Wind, Snake, and Bonnet Plume, which flow north to the Peel.

Bonnet Plume:
Homeland of the Loucheux

BY C.E.S. FRANKS

Unlike more famous northern rivers, the Bonnet Plume is associated with no history of exploration or legends of great and tragic deeds. It is one of the hundreds of small rivers that flow through the Canadian wilderness, hardly touched by man. It is also one of the most beautiful. From its source high in the mountains of the Continental Divide, it flows due north through the Yukon until it meets the Peel. The first 150 miles from the put-in at Bonnet Plume Lake are in a narrow valley between mountains. Then the relief becomes lower, the valley wider. The river drops more than 10 feet per mile, making it fast and, potentially, very dangerous.

It took two trips for an Otter to carry six of us, our gear, and three canoes from Mayo in the Yukon to Bonnet Plume Lake. I arrived on the second trip, with Shawn Hodgins and Saundra Raymond, after nine in the evening. The mountains surrounding the lake were speckled with light and shadow, set off by towering cumulus clouds. Peter Milliken and Bob and Helene Edwards had gone in on the first flight. Tents were set up near an outfitter's camp; grayling and lake trout fillets were frying for dinner.

We would spend two days beside the lake hiking, fishing, and taking in the scenery before starting down the river on our 323-mile journey to Fort McPherson, near the Peel/Mackenzie confluence. While camped, we met two other wilderness travelers, who had flown in a few days earlier. They were to catch up with the other two of their crew in a day or so. As it turned out, our pace on the river was about the same, and we met each other frequently at camps, on rapids, or on the water. They were good company and didn't make the river crowded.

Another meeting came on our second day at the campsite. Shawn and I were fishing for grayling in the creek that flows from the lake to the Bonnet Plume River. The fishing was almost too good. I was catching a feisty little grayling with nearly every fly cast. This soon gave me more than we needed and was becoming boring. I heard some noise, and looked up to see a dog (at first I thought it was a wolf) and three men on horseback. They were guides, bringing in horses and supplies to the outfitters' camp for the hunting season.

They had ridden in from Macmillan Pass, more than 90 miles to the south, near the headwaters of the Nahanni. It had taken them twelve days to make

The Bonnet Plume rises high in the Mackenzie Mountains of the Continental Divide, dropping 300 feet in 329 miles.

Overleaf: *Campfire pans on the Bonnet Plume are often filled with fillets of arctic grayling, a small yet feisty fish. The milky color of the water in this photograph is due to silt from mountain glaciers.*

the trip. The outfitter they work for has rights to 4,325 square miles of mountain country, and during the eight-week season they host up to four trophy hunters at a time, who fly in on two-week hunts for moose, caribou, bear, or Dall's sheep. The hunters pay up to $10,000 each; to the guides, who go back south to Alberta and California after the season ends, the two-month stay in the Yukon is a paid vacation.

The guides soon had a spotting scope out, and in short order we were all watching a sow grizzly and her cub hunting for ground squirrels on a mountainside several miles away. These bears hibernate for eight months of the year, the guides told us.

Next morning we had a relaxed cup of coffee with the guides, said our good-byes, and began down the river. We were a little apprehensive because we'd heard reports of a challenging run through a huge mud and rock slide that filled the valley. Centuries ago, the river had carved a 2-mile piece off the face of the mountains. (The previous year, one crew had taken two days to get through and had suffered a very dangerous capsize.) The photos we'd seen didn't make the river look as difficult as that, but we were still a little nervous. I think even the best canoeists are mildly nervous at the beginning of a long trip on a strange river. You never know what lies ahead. And tales of the horrors and terrors others have experienced don't reduce the nervousness.

We came to the gorge after an hour of paddling. The day was sunny and warm. As we entered it we kept our ears open for the deeper sound of impassable rapids or waterfalls, but we didn't hear it. We hugged the inner shore as the river meandered around innumerable bends, and we scouted one piece from a ledge. An hour later we were at the end. No problems. Elated. Ran everything else until we camped beside a small creek 19 miles from where we'd begun. Pizza for dinner and rum toddies for comfort and cheer.

In its first 62 miles, the Bonnet Plume crashes through four canyons. Choosing not to shoot canyon rapids can lead to another set of little problems.

The next two days followed the same pattern. Spectacular scenery, many sets of Class II and III rapids, a few short portages, a meeting with our fellow travelers.

On the fourth day we reached the canyon that was supposed to require a 1-mile portage. We had seen slides of a friend's trip on the Bonnet Plume, replete with dumps in cold, formidable-looking water, anxiety about making the schedule, bad weather, and twenty-hour days to make up lost time. Some of us had also seen a TV film of a cold, miserable-looking crew traveling down the

Left: *On the edge of the tree line, the Bonnet Plume provides excellent opportunities for hiking.*

Below: *Members of Franks's expedition shoot a set of rapids on the Bonnet Plume.*

same river and obviously having great difficulty handling the rapids.

Sometimes we wondered whether we were on the right river. Here we were at a "compulsory" portage around one of the most difficult rapids. We looked it over. The river was in a deep gorge, but we scrambled along the bank and found that, after a first short piece of dangerous, rock-filled rapids, there was an exciting Class III rapid, a short carry, and then what looked like an easy run out to the end. Shawn, the youngest of us at twenty-three but also the best white-water canoeist, had pointed out that if we crossed to the far side at the top we had only to lift our canoes over a small drop; then we could run the rapids down to the carry around the falls.

Two of our canoes did this. The third elected to portage. We found it wasn't all that simple, requiring precise maneuvering in the heavy water and a careful eddy turn and landing above the falls. The party we were sharing the river with also ran. One of them hit a rock and got unpleasantly full of water; but they too managed to pull out.

We sat in the bright sunlight and had lunch, the sparkle of the mist from the falls behind us, their quiet roar a constant background sound. A grayling, curious about the intrusion, came up to the surface of the milky water and sampled some crumbs. We examined the Mad River ABS canoe that had banged the rock and found a tear in the tough outer vinyl. Nothing serious, but more damage than expected.

This was the end of the difficult water. All we had to do from now on was stay on the river: the current would get us to the end, even if we hardly lifted a paddle. We now had a week of comfortable, relaxed canoeing to get to Fort McPherson. The river was ours to enjoy.

On every canoe trip there is a time when you begin to come to terms with a river. Each river has its own character. Some are unfriendly and have long, hard portages and sparse, stunted fish; others are idyllic and easy. The Bonnet Plume, we had learned, was not a difficult river, though it did require careful judgment and decisive maneuvering. It was running at a good speed and would take us where we wanted with little effort. The snow-topped mountains, a wooded river valley, the full bloom of the wildflowers of arctic summer, and plentiful fish and wildlife were spectacular. The weather, which is much more fickle in these mountains of the Yukon than on the Barren Lands to the east of the Mackenzie River, had been mostly good. We and the river were on good terms,

and there appeared to be no reason for us not to remain so.

As we neared the end of yet another canyon, a huge bald eagle flew up from a gravel bar. A good omen. During the following days there was some rain, but most of the time it was sunny with enough wind to keep the bugs down. I used bug repellent only three times during the trip. One day after lunch we saw seven white Dall's sheep winding their way around the mountainside 900 feet above us. Another day a woodland caribou with a magnificent set of antlers came to inspect our campsite. Once, a wolf kept watch on us for a while, and soon afterward a moose ambled away through the bush at a pace a man couldn't match.

We were beginning to leave the cares of the south behind us. For the first days we'd slept ten to twelve hours. Now we were down to eight. The river broadened, and the mountains grew lower and more distant. As we approached the Peel River, nine days after landing at Bonnet Plume Lake, the river divided into many channels in a 10-mile-long delta of rocks and gravel. The river here was very fast. I measured its speed one morning at 6 miles per hour as it streamed past the campsite. It stayed fast as it rushed down the delta, zigzagging from side to side like a skier traversing to slow a steep descent.

Normally a canoeist is at the lowest point of a valley. If you can't see what's ahead, you feel uneasy. If you see a horizon line across the river you feel more than uneasy; you stop and look. On these last miles of the Bonnet Plume we could see the river dropping as it raced ahead of us. But we could also see a horizon line to the side, where the delta dropped faster than the river. This isn't normal. I kept expecting the river to fall off; but it never did, and soon we reached the Peel.

It was browner than the Bonnet Plume, and at times we could hear a sound like light rain on a tent; it was silt hitting the bottom of the canoe. Not all wilderness rivers are clear, and I had to remind myself that one should not make the mistake of assuming nature never erodes or pollutes. The Peel soon entered a gorge with 500-foot cliffs lining a winding channel. A little care was needed to avoid the heavy standing waves, but we spent more time marveling at the cliffs than worrying about the rapids.

As we rounded that last bend we were hit full in the face by a fierce headwind; so, even though it was only 3:00 p.m., we retreated behind the shelter of the last point of the canyon cliffs and camped. The site was sheltered from the wind but exposed enough to keep the mosquitoes at bay. We sunbathed, swam, washed, and caught grayling for our last fish dinner. The water was 55°F. After dinner we climbed to the top of the cliff to admire the spectacular view up the river through the canyon and beyond.

Two days later, as the Peel worked its way north, we camped at the Arctic Circle. The next day we met Neil Colin, a Loucheux Indian from Fort McPherson, and his son Dempster. We had arranged for them to take us, our canoes and gear by riverboat over the last, slow 68 miles of the Peel. As we motored along, Neil pointed out the features of the river—the ancient portages and summer fishing camps. There was some southerners' history, too, the sites where the bodies of the Lost Patrol had been found. This unfortunate RCMP patrol refused the help of native guides and lost their way going from Dawson to Fort McPherson in 1911.

McPherson is a quiet Indian village. We pitched our tents near Neil's summer camp on the shores of the Peel where the Dempster Highway ferry crosses the river on its way to Inuvik. When we had finished dinner and were ready for the sleeping bags, it was 1:00 a.m. and still light. The huskies chained at the camps along the river sang us to sleep and awoke us again near dawn, when they howled in unison at a fire siren sounding in the village.

The next morning we stored our rented canoes at Neil's camp; they would be picked up by the outfitter in Whitehorse. We breakfasted and packed at a leisurely pace. Bob and Helene decided to hitchhike to Whitehorse; Shawn and Saundra got a ride on the Dempster-to-Inuvik with a tourist from Chicago.

Peter and I visited Neil and had coffee. We met his wife, Elizabeth, and sampled some fish he'd smoked; they had been netted in the river. Elizabeth's mother, Mary, joined us. She made her living through the hard work of smoke-tanning moosehides. She had been born eighty years earlier, in the mountains we had canoed through. Neil told us the Loucheux names of some of the hills, valleys, cliffs, and rivers we had passed that were nameless on the map. I learned that "Bonnet Plume" is the English translation of an Indian name, and that many Bonnet Plume families lived in Fort McPherson.

I was wrong in thinking that the river had no history or legends; it has. But the legends belong to the Loucheux Indians, and the history is of their thousands of years of hunting, fishing, and cultural development; not of recent white intruders. Our wilderness was their homeland. Their history may die as the Indians lose their culture—the dog belonging to Neil and Elizabeth's grandson was named Michael Jackson—but this history is still there, though neglected. It is not yet too late for it to be made part of our understanding and knowledge.

Left: *Early-morning sun catches the bright reds and yellows of canoes and canoeists as they break camp for another day's run.*

Below: *End of a journey. The Peel River near Fort McPherson. Buoys mark the top of a whitefish net tended by local Loucheux Indians.*

I realize that this tale of the Bonnet Plume doesn't have the drama, tension, or excitement of many descriptions of northern river traveling. Partly, I think, this is because some descriptions of pretty uneventful trips are dramatized—"colored," as my friend Eric Morse says—to give them a spurious element of adventure and fearfulness. But there are two other reasons. First, the Bonnet Plume tales we'd heard proved that a wild-river experience can be very difficult for canoeists unfamiliar with reading rapids and white-water maneuvers. We had the experience and skill to see us through with ease; but, more important, we weren't looking for difficulty and adventure. The trip was a chance to get close to nature and to change the pace of our lives; we didn't want excessive stress and pressure. We got what we wanted—two weeks of fabulous scenery and wildlife, excellent canoeing, the company of friends, and a chance to get body, mind, and soul together in the healing northern canoe country.

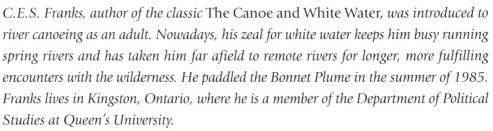

C.E.S. Franks, author of the classic The Canoe and White Water, *was introduced to river canoeing as an adult. Nowadays, his zeal for white water keeps him busy running spring rivers and has taken him far afield to remote rivers for longer, more fulfilling encounters with the wilderness. He paddled the Bonnet Plume in the summer of 1985. Franks lives in Kingston, Ontario, where he is a member of the Department of Political Studies at Queen's University.*

The South Nahanni River is the centerpiece of Nahanni National Park, which includes 1,815 square miles of mountains, wild rivers, hot springs, and big-game habitat in the south-west corner of the Northwest Territories.

CHAPTER EIGHT

Protected Wild

There is no Canadian wild river that has attracted more interest and attention than the legendary Nahanni. Much of the river is now within the boundaries of a national park. Features such as the 328-foot Virginia Falls, hot springs, tufa mounds, spectacular canyons, and mountain scenery prompted the United Nations Educational, Scientific, and Cultural Organization (UNESCO) to designate Nahanni National Park the first World Heritage Site.

Nahanni: River of Gold

BY WALLY SCHABER

Trip notes invariably say something dry like "the headwaters of the South Nahanni River are marked by a pair of shallow lakes at the foot of Mount Wilson." This might make sense in your living room, but when the plane banks to land in the shadow of Wilson, the notes don't come close to what the Nahanni source is really like. The Moose Ponds, as they are affectionately called, seem barely big enough to float a canoe—let alone a plane—but it is here that one of life's very special experiences begins.

The upper Nahanni is a superb wild river. I began guiding canoe trips on the Nahanni in 1976; my rough census indicates that approximately a dozen groups have begun at the Moose Ponds each year since 1981; there was about half that number between 1976 and 1981. Prior to the mid-1970s, only a handful of parties began their canoe journey of discovery right at the source. (After consulting local air charter services and outfitters, you can still find a starting date that will ensure that you have the river all to yourself.)

R.M. Patterson's book, *The Dangerous River*, peaked my interest in the Nahanni. He lived it! I learned from Patterson that all the early prospectors discovered gold—of a sort—on this wild mountain river. I'm convinced that Nahanni riches are not so much in elusive nuggets as in doing, seeing, and being part of a river adventure.

My Nahanni experiences begin with hiking boots, not neoprene socks. I take a lunch and a map to the top of Mount Wilson. Wilson's 3,500-foot height above the Moose Ponds translates into a five-hour hike to mountain panorama.

To the north are the snow-capped peaks of the Itse Range along which the Ross River flows. A 5-mile portage links this river and the Canol Road with the Moose Ponds, making it a Nahanni access alternative for those with more time and muscle than flight money. A little farther to the north, just off the map and out of sight, are the headwaters of the Bonnet Plume, Keele, and Mountain rivers. Directly east is O'Grady Lake, source of the Natla River. To the west are the

Below Third Canyon and upriver from Second Canyon is Pulpit Rock, a favored hiking place for Nahanni canoeists. This unusual feature sometimes called "The Gates of the Nahanni" was formed at an oxbow, when water eroded a straighter path to the sea, leaving a dry channel and a lone spire of rock.

A Single Otter floatplane lands author Schaber and company in the Moose Ponds. To the south is majestic Mount Wilson.

Selwyn Mountains that define the Yukon/Northwest Territories border. And to the south, the Nahanni. From Wilson it looks like little more than a meandering creek with tiny patches of white water.

The view from Wilson may be seductive, but it is deceptive: people without two or three years of Class III river running should stay atop Wilson! In the 44 miles between the Moose Ponds and the junction of the Little Nahanni River, the Nahanni drops 980 feet—a stretch of formidable rapids.

This segment of the Nahanni, dubbed the Rock Garden, is river-running heaven, an experience pristine and personal. It is tempting, however, to rush the river and to run rapids all day, every day. This can be a costly mistake. Time must be taken to assess the variables: the water is cold, the days are long, and canoe loads are at their heaviest. Moreover, you usually have yet to perfect your paddling teamwork, and the most challenging portion of the river is farthest from help. There are plenty of campsites. Everything suggests a slow, relaxed pace and that's exactly how successful parties do it.

Rapids get more difficult as the river progresses. The first day downstream from the Moose Ponds is mostly Class I rapids, although I have had the odd moose or caribou provide a moving obstacle in this section. The second day, tributaries swell the river, making it Class II in dry weather and tricky Class III if it is rainy. During days 3 and 4 in the Rock Garden, exciting rapids appear in long runs with short pools between. Usually there is just enough time to bail and to congratulate one another. I've often been thankful for ABS plastic canoes that are most forgiving when it comes to sliding around and over rounded boulders.

The Rock Garden has claimed at least one life. In high water, rapids like Initiation, Tributary, Hollywood, and Big Bend, without marked portages, often prove too much for loaded canoes and inexperienced paddlers. Lining is always an option, but I have found it difficult to pinpoint position on 1:250,000 topographic maps (at present the only scale available). I have relied most often on caution and common sense to make it safely down the upper river.

There is no better way to end the rocking and rolling of the upper Nahanni than to languish in a natural hot tub! I think often of lying in the first of three Nahanni hot springs, pushing a floating tray of *hors d'oeuvres* back and forth in the water while toasting deeds of skill and daring in the Rock Garden.

Silt-laden waters of Bologna Creek enter the Nahanni below the Rock Garden and begin to cloud the crystal-clear mountain waters of the upper Nahanni. At

Opposite: *Nahanni, the River of Gold,*
with its prize nugget, Virginia Falls—twice
as high as Niagara.

Below: *Quiet times.*

The Nahanni valley's fabled cliffs rise above the campsite of a Nahanni river-runner.

Beneath a spray cover, warmly dressed paddlers concentrate on finding a safe route through the treacherous "Rock Garden."

Even the roughest, wildest rivers have stretches of tranquil
water. Here sun and hills are reflected on the Nahanni.

this point the river is moving along at 5 to 10 miles per hour; with only Class II Elbow rapids to break the ride, you can float 50 miles a day on this magic carpet. However, I have always interpreted the silt as a signal that the river valley now has more to say than the river itself.

Below the confluence of the Little Nahanni and the South Nahanni, the entire river can be negotiated by paddlers with only Class I experience. In fact, it is probably more important to be a good hiker than a good paddler for the lower three-quarters of the river.

Hiking is most accessible and enjoyable around the cabin built in the summer of 1978 by newlyweds John and Joanne Moore, as their base for a winter of wilderness living. Their book, *Nahanni Trailhead*, enriches hiking in the area. At their suggestion, I've trekked to alpine meadows high above the river; I've even stumbled on an old horse trail leading back to the Little Nahanni valley.

Down river, 10 tough miles due west, hides the jewel of the Ragged Mountain Range. Shimmering Glacier Lake is surrounded by the highest peaks in the Northwest Territories: MacBrien, Smith, Ida, and Mount Sidney Dobson (8,635 feet). There is a meadow at the base of these giants, "The Cirque of the Unclimbables," that is pure magic: sheer granite above, glacier-capped peaks in the distance, opal-green lake below, yesterday's Nahanni valley stretching out of sight to the north and tomorrow's river to the south—and all of this shrouded in wilderness silence.

An hour of drifting from the Glacier Creek campsite brings you to a large yellow sign that announces, "You are now entering Nahanni National Park." This park was established in 1976 to protect the treasures of the Nahanni. The sign means your personal freedom and wilderness experience will be managed to some degree.

How you accept the park and what it stands for depends largely on your philosophy of wilderness preservation. Whatever your feelings, a stop at the park warden's cabin to exchange stories and have a swim in the clear, warm waters of nearby Rabbitkettle Lake is well worthwhile. I always look forward to an invitation from the warden for a guided day trip to Rabbitkettle Hot Springs.

This natural phenomenon is one of the special features that helped the Nahanni gain national-park status. Rabbitkettle Hot Springs figured prominently, too, in UNESCO's designation of the Nahanni region as a "World Heritage Site" in 1979. The hot springs are so fragile that wardens insist boots be

The "Sluice Box"—one of the Nahanni's most dangerous sections of white water.

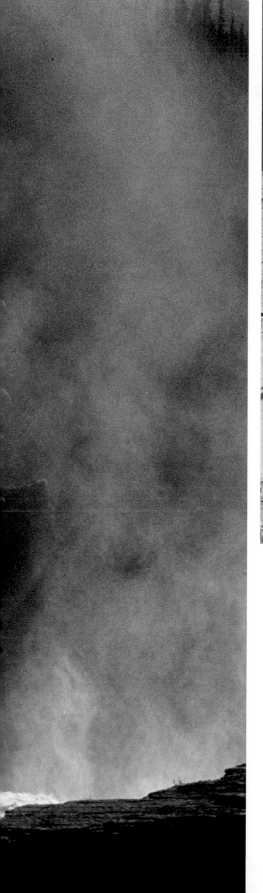

Nahanni: River of Gold 127

removed when approaching this chalky yellowish-gray structure that stands 98 feet high and 199 feet wide.

"This mound grows at a rate of one-tenth of an inch per year," a warden explains. "You are looking at ten thousand years of nature's handiwork." On tiptoes we climb to a top pool. The 70°F water is crystal clear and slowly overflows in several directions. The warden explains that dissolved minerals, mostly calcium, precipitate and form small terraces that in turn divert the direction of the overflow. In this manner, over centuries, the hot spring has grown to a circular tufa mound. One slip of the foot of a careless bather or enthusiastic photographer could damage a century of nature's labor!

The showpiece of the park is Virginia Falls, Canada's highest. About 9 miles above this impressive, 328-foot cataract, the river slows down and meanders, almost teasing. Closer to the falls, the power of the river becomes dangerously hypnotic. I've stood mesmerized at Sluice Box, a Class VI rapid just above the falls, and imagined enough tongues, eddies, and escape islands to make it through in a canoe. Trouble is, Sluice Box ends in an explosion! Water jets 30 to 50 feet in all directions as if struggling to avoid the brink. A 100-foot spire of limestone somehow resists all this force and divides the river into a major and minor curtain. There is a treacherous ledge right at water level, where the view of the brink is breathtaking. Fortunately, the park people have established a campsite a safe distance away from the falls and have built a boardwalk that guides visitors to many lookout points.

Directly below the falls is Fourth Canyon. Early Nahanni travelers, such as the legendary Albert Faillie and the unfortunate McLeod brothers (found *sans* heads in what is now known as Deadmen Valley), poled and tracked their way upstream for a first view of Virginia Falls. They numbered three canyons below the falls in ascending order. Rolling waves and violent shoreline eddies, combined with 10- to 12-mile-per hour current, make the descent of 5-mile First Canyon very exciting. When I suggest to most people that they secure their spray skirts for this section of river, I always remember that the prospectors negotiated the river in open skiffs.

Even wilder than Fourth Canyon is Hell's Gate. A stubborn limestone cliff forces the river to take an abrupt left turn, creating two whirlpools with a nasty boil and a ridge of standing waves in the middle. The safest route through is the line of standing waves; but when caution prevails, I've seen paddlers portage along the downstream cliff on a trail that provides excellent canyon viewing.

The Nahanni valley is one of the few areas of Canada to have escaped the effects of the last ice age. Ten thousand years of current have cut a spectacular incision into the Mackenzie Mountains. It's pure heaven floating past the various highlights: Flat River, Third Canyon, Pulpit Rock, Big Bend, Second Canyon, and Deadmen Valley.

If the ill-fated McLeod brothers had not lost their heads, Deadmen Valley could well be called Paradise. The opportunities for exploring, fishing, photography, and relaxation are bountiful. Patterson describes spirited adventures he and his partner had in places such as Prairie Creek, Dry Canyon, Tlogotsho Plateau, and above First Canyon.

First Canyon is the deepest and most spectacular of all. George's Riffle blocks the entrance of this 3,208-foot canyon with diagonal, rolling waves and unpredictable haystacks. Many an intrepid voyageur who has not scouted the Riffle has been in for a rough ride and, on occasion, a very cold swim! The walls of First Canyon are marked by dark entrances to craters and caves in the porous limestone. In the 1960s, exploration of one of these caves led to the discovery of nearly 100 Dall's sheep skeletons. The Valerie Caves are now closed to the public to allow for preservation and further study.

But you must concentrate on the water: Lafferty's Riffle is coming up, the last hurrah for the Nahanni traveler before a day's journey brings you to the village of Nahanni Butte, the Liard River, and civilization. Large standing waves bounce happy crews along the outside of the last curve of First Canyon, and then the Nahanni rests.

Memories of last nights on many Nahanni trips include the sun setting over the rim of First Canyon as companions share the last rum rations and soak in a final hot spring. Toasts often echo R.M. Patterson's words, which sum up my feelings for the Nahanni: "The treasure is in the adventure. Let's not destroy the adventure for those who follow by taking the wild out of wilderness."

After long involvement in camp canoeing in Ontario, Wally Schaber founded Black Feather Wilderness Adventures in the early 1970s. Since then, he and his staff have guided thousands of people on expeditions in Canada's premier wild lands. He is as comfortable in Newfoundland as he is on Baffin Island or Kluane, but he is most at home in a canoe, having paddled just about all major Canadian canoe routes. Schaber lives in Ottawa, where he is co-owner of Trail Head, an adventure-sport organization with retail stores in Ottawa and Toronto.

Tufa mound at Rabbitkettle Hot Springs—ten thousand years of nature's handiwork.

Hiking up Sheaf Creek to the alpine meadows of the Tlogotsho Plateau is a difficult three-to-five-day side trip in the vicinity of First Canyon and Deadmen Valley. Ambitious ramblers are rewarded with breathtaking views of the river.

Chalk Basin is a spectacular "wedding cake" formation along Oregon's remote Owyhee River.

CHAPTER NINE

Continental Wild

From the St. John, Delaware, Pee Dee, and Peace in the populous East, to the Heartland's Niobrara, Black, and Bayou Penchant, southwest to the canyons of the Rio Grande, Escalante, Purgatoire, and Colorado, and up to the Tuolumne, Carson, Salmon, Smith, Rogue, and Skagit in the great Northwest, the continental United States is blessed with a stunning diversity of rivers protected by the 1983 Wild and Scenic River Act. Each of these nourishes its own ecology and informs the lives of the people who live in its watershed. Each river has its history, its joys and conflicts. The Owyhee is no exception. Tucked into southeastern Oregon, a tributary of the mighty Snake, the Owyhee is emblematic of a river across the nation, of interest when the water is high and raging, quiet and unpeopled for the rest of the year. Having rafted this river many times as a professional guide, Melinda Allan returned at low water with her husband, Al Law, and, traveling in small inflatable canoes, discovered a river again, for the first time.

Paddling in Paradise: Oregon's Remote Owyhee Canyonlands

BY MELINDA ALLAN

T ime to play human pinball again! Quick backward strokes of the double-bladed paddle stall my inflatable canoe, allowing a few more seconds to appraise the situation. Like most steep rapids, "Bull's-Eye" remains invisible to boaters seated at water level until the very last moment. Staring down into a maze of boulders and spray, I suddenly realize that no clear route exists. Then the current grabs hold of my little boat.

Windmilling my paddle sends the inflatable canoe flying into the only open water, a slim slot on the far left side, barely clearing a pair of boulders. True to the rapid's name, the current slams hard into another boulder smack in the middle of the river. A quick turn avoids this hazard, but dumps my boat sideways over a kitchen sink–sized rock. Leaning hard downstream, bracing with the paddle, means I escape with only my boat swamped and my dignity dampened. The canoe is waterlogged only for a moment before the self-bailer drains water out through four holes carved in the fabric floor. Able to maneuver again, I arrive at the bottom of my first technical Class IV rapid upright—although unceremoniously backwards.

A merry ride, typical of the rapids that my husband, Al Law, and I will encounter while running this remote desert river by ourselves at extremely low water levels. We laugh and shout in victory, our exuberance tempered by a firm decision to scout the next major drop from shore, where the view is better, the surface not moving you closer every moment. Although we have rammed rocks, wiggled through passages almost too tight to accommodate our yard-wide boats, and dragged over gravel bars, these tough, bullet-shaped inflatable canoes remain undamaged.

Paddling isn't usually this tiring, but today we've pushed extra miles. Last night's camp was on a sloped sand dune, and about 3:30 A.M., we discovered why the sands were so perfectly sculpted: the canyon was a natural funnel for fierce upstream winds that blew grit into our faces and tossed our supplies across the river. I scrambled naked in the predawn starlight to save our boats from being blown away, even though they were weighed down with gear. The wind was STRONG. Later, we scavenged across the canyon for lost water jugs and other lightweight items. Thankfully, nothing important was lost.

We sought refuge from thunderstorms inside a big cave at river level.

In higher water levels, rafters approach the "Gates" of Montgomery Gorge, which seems to swallow them into its depths.

Wildlife includes birds of prey like this baby great horned owl (bottom)
and lizards of all kinds (top).

Once the hurricane abates, and we reach the current, things are better. We giggle like children, teasing each other about being the "probe boat" that goes first, leaving the other with a clear view of where *not* to go. The problem is, we've never seen this river below a water level of 1,000 cubic feet per second. This time out, the level is 190 at Rome, Oregon, the lowest-ever run that we know about. The rangers thoughtfully put up a warning sign to keep kooks like us from doing this kind of thing. But here we are, professional river guides getting a little bored with the approach of middle age, looking to be kids again.

This remote river where we "guide" greenhorns has, in the absence of roaring water, become a mysterious passage; our favorite campsites are still there, as are our rock-hounding places and hiking trails. Only the river looks radically different. Unlike the rollick and wash of the river a few seasons back, when El Niño brought a flood to the desert, making this a rafts-only river, today we're in technical, rocky water that is ideal for our inflatables. And we're having a blast! There's nothing like pushing your little boat off into the unknown, the mystery of rapids ahead not really understood, that quickens the adrenalin in our blood. We are explorers—Huck Finn and Tom Sawyer (or at least Becky Thatcher)—out to tame the Mississippi. Lewis and Sacajawea. Maybe Bonnie and Clyde? River rebels!

I feel the wind-lengthened day drag on as a bright June afternoon turns cool. We can camp almost anywhere except where we are now, a tight basalt-rock gorge with no flat shorelines. Hot springs! We stop at Upset Rapid, but it's gone at this water level, and its warm spring is only 70°F, barely warmer than the river at this level. Instead of a hot springs, we ward off the cool breeze by taking small waves sideways, splashing that tepid river water over chilled thighs. Paddling jackets help ward off the wind, and I am beginning to master the double-bladed paddle at last, thanks to the wind. (I started with the blades unfeathered, but quickly understood the advantages gained in having the non-power surface flat to the wind.) Confidence builds as the heat we generate from paddling warms our upper bodies, warding off dangerous hypothermia, always a problem in Oregon, even on a sunny June afternoon in the desert.

Finally we reach the hot-springs camp, a small beach below a noisy riffle. The riffle is caused by a geologic-fault upheaval, where the hot steam breaks the ground all across the river, creating a ledge where we could play in surf all day if we were up to the challenge. Darkness comes rapidly in a deep river canyon; Al scurries around, getting the tent up—"No more sleeping out, no more sand in my face, no more wind!"—finishing the chore quickly while I concoct a backpacker-style meal.

Soon, tense shoulder muscles are soothed by one of nature's most marvelous creations, the wilderness hot spring, as I ease into the delightful 103°F water. As I soak, the night deepens. We listen to the music of the river. Above us flows a river of stars, rimmed by black canyon walls. Somewhere, a great horned owl begins hooting.

The river is a magical place, a place that may attract several thousand other boaters every spring during a short but intense float season. But, for the next week, we won't see another person—two second-honeymooners in a desert canyon, alone on a river journey, as we guide our inflatables downstream. On this trip, the big cave will be untrammeled, the next hot-springs camp also empty, and the fish still hungry.

Drought throughout the West has altered the float plans of many parties; abysmally low water levels bar the use of traditional river craft. But I have faith in the tough little cocoon of fabric, coating, and air-insulating my body, as I must, for the nearest road is 40 miles away, beyond perpendicular rock walls. Many rapids will be like Bull's-Eye—tight and rocky, barely wide enough for the inflatables to wiggle through—and in a few places we'll be forced to carry for safety. There will be a million razor-edged rocks, impossible to dodge them all—so I crash into them, and keep on going. A few years ago, such a journey would have been impossible.

Rafts attempting to float this scenic stretch would have been stranded in shallows around the first bend of the river. Older inflatables made of cheap, thin materials would have been torn to shreds. Canoes and hardshell kayaks would take a beating, would never carry us through the tight passages with the hundred pounds of food and gear we have stowed behind our seats, and these craft might prove dangerous if tipped over in low water. That Bureau of Land Management warning sign means business! However, my 10-foot long inflatable can thread and wiggle through narrow slots much more easily than a 17-foot canoe or even a 12-foot kayak. Only our modern inflatable canoes make this expedition possible, or practical.

We leave the hot-springs camp with reluctance, paddling like demons as a thunderstorm gathers overhead. Shelter lies ahead in the form of a cave as big as a three-room house, but first we must cope with Whistling Bird Rapid, the worst rapid on the Owyhee at low water.

The rapid is different at this tiny flow. Instead of pouring into a cliff wall and sucking into an underwater cover, the current slams into a rock with a log pinned and held there. Al takes his larger boat through first, clearing this ugly obstacle by mere inches, despite his powerful, sure strokes. Frantic whistle-blowing stops my run, though. Al walks back, white-faced. "Let's walk," he says, indicating with two fingers that he came much closer to the log than he cared to. I gladly tie a lining rope to my boat.

The thunderstorm strikes with full force as we lurch into the cave, high and dry. We watch a stream of white fluid run down from the Chalk Basin and cloud the Owyhee until the desert stream looks like a bowl of 2% milk with Cheerios logs floating in eddies. I catch a couple of catfish and bass in the eddy during a clearing in the storm, then set up kitchen and stove at the mouth of the cave, using a stone slab for a picnic table. "You look like Wilma Flintstone," Al says, grinning. "And you're Fred," I counter, pointing at Al's generous midsection. He chases me to the river's edge as I scoop up water for cleaning. Drinking water we get from the hundreds of new springs we've discovered that exist below the normal level of the river, including one back at Whistling Bird—the terrifying cove that

Like a huge Easter Island statue, we felt the watchful eyes of "The Sentinel" upon us as we traversed the last canyon before journey's end.

has been known to kill several boaters at higher flows is now a drip cave, replete with mosses and fresh water. Most of the springs we find are warm, over 70°F, but not many are hot springs, which are usually over 100°F.

We stay at the cave two days, reading tales of adventure, or just lying on our stomachs and watching the restless clouds roll past, dumping rain. The river's too murky now for fishing, so we're back to civilized food—macaroni and cheese, and canned fish.

We paddle ahead, leaving the sanctuary of the cave behind, mindful of our minimal food supplies. Without fish we can't linger too long in one place. We have planned for a week's outing and, besides our food supply, must remember our rendezvous with my in-laws and their powerboat at the head of the lake in a few days.

Suddenly, the "Gates of the Owyhee" loom ahead, forbidding red walls that rise a thousand feet straight from the water's edge, sheer and spectacular, awesome and inviting … yet a chill creeps down my spine. Somewhere in that great basalt-rock gorge lies Iron Point Rapid, one of the toughest sections of white water on our float. Tightening cliffs engulf us, devour our horizons,

delivering us and our little boats into this narrow chasm of rock and river.

Bull's-Eye was an unknown, a rapid we'd never seen at low water, so we're cautious at Iron Point. But this trip will be different. After dodging through Rock Trap and other small riffles, Iron Point is a splash-and-giggle run. The current is still moving hard toward the "wrap rocks" on the far left, but with the shallows we can cheat to the right, using our now patented and famous "One Rock Stop"—hit a rock hard, get stuck, laugh, and wiggle our behinds to get the boats loose, then paddle hard to the next rock. The rapids where we expect trouble have been nothing, except for Whistling Bird. The little-known ones are trashing us.

There are so many favorite places along this 65-mile stretch of river and lake headwaters that I can't decide on the best spot to be. Surely at the top ranks Montgomery Gorge (also called Green Dragon Canyon, although it's red, not green, and there are no dragons, just bighorn sheep and golden eagles soaring overhead). Right up there are the hot springs where we stay our last two nights, first at Greeley Bar, then at the head of the Owyhee Reservoir. The colors of the Owyhee Canyon must be seen to be believed, as must the intricate patterns of the badlands and gulches—Chalk Basin, Lambert Rocks, Leslie Gulch. Like a combination of Bryce Canyon, Zion, and maybe even Salvador Dali, this country cries out for Kodachrome film. but even the best film can't capture all the mystery, for which I'm glad.

That last night out is even better than the first hot springs, because some thoughtful powerboater has made a *shower* there, using old PVC pipe. Talk about shower massages! The lake is otherwise dull, long paddling through mudflats now that the water level is so low (and the best reason to use a motor whenever the weather allows!). I lag far behind Al, whose powerful long arms stroke his longer boat and greater weight with ease. I am in tears by the time I hit the lake and finally catch a glimpse of him far ahead. Tears then turn to sulfur steam as I strip and dive into the hot pool, then try out the never-ending 104°F shower.

Another favorite place is the Native American petroglyphs found along the Owyhee. But I feel a lump in my throat writing about them because vandals have desecrated this fragile site, chipping away some of my favorite scenes to take home as souvenirs. I breathe a sigh of relief as I once again locate my favorite bighorn ram, near a mosaic of Stone Age hunters. This "glyph" must have been powerful magic in those days, luring the spirit of the sheep to the flimsy bows that kept those nomadic peoples alive in this raw desert.

I love knowing the history of this spectacular country, too. The big Owyhee country is more than just pretty scenery, it's people and their stories as well, from those first sagebrush-sandaled primitives to the fur trappers and home-steaders, to moonshiners and pioneer river guides like Oregon's Prince Helfrich. Every rock tells a story, too, even the ones we make up on the spot.

Many people are thrilled just to learn that the name "Owyhee" (pronounced *Oh-why-hee*) really does derive from Hawaii. Back in 1818, fur trapper and explorer Donald McKenzie led an expedition to the Snake River area. Upon encountering the Owyhee tributary, two Hawaiians, or "Owyhees," who were with the expedi-tion were sent upstream to investigate the beaver supply. They never returned.

What happened to them? Most historians believe that they were killed by the Snake Indians, a fierce tribe who didn't care for intruders of any race. A few oldtimers will tell you the Hawaiians were captured alive, and that if you scout the remote outbacks, you can still find Hawaiian-style petroglyphs. A romantic mystery, to be sure, but considering another ill-fated pair, the Jordan brothers, who came here to prospect for gold and were found, not just murdered, but "so cut to pieces that they had to bundle them up in a blanket just to bury them," our minds boggled as we considered the possibilities.

Modern adventurers don't have to worry about attacks by savages or bandits, just hypothermia, rattlesnakes, heat stroke, drought, rocks, rapids, and hurri-cane winds. Despite the risks, though, the Owyhee remains a special place to me, one I'll always treasure. Designated as a national Wild and Scenic River, the Owyhee will remain forever wild, so boaters can continue to float its cur-rents into Paradise, just as I did. And I'll be back next spring. Please, though, let's have higher water levels!

Melinda Allan is a professional river guide and freelance writer who has traveled and written about many river routes in Oregon, the state that boasts more Wild and Scenic Rivers than any other. In addition to writing for magazines and books, she is a regular outdoor columnist for the The Register-Guard *in Eugene, Oregon. Ms. Allan lives in Creswell, Oregon, with her husband, Al Law, and together they operate Al's Wild Water Adventures, an outfitting firm that offers a wide range of river trips in the Pacific Northwest.*

Previous spread: *Towering cliffs in Sentinel Canyon are transformed into a magnificent display of color and light as the sun sets.*

Photo Credits

Melinda Allan, 134–135, 136–137, 138–139, 143, 144–145

Dave Babbitt, 14–15, 20, 21, 28–29, 30

Mike Beedell, x–xi, xiv, 3, 4–5, 8, 11, 12, 118–119, 122

Fraser Clarke, 98–99, 102, 104, 106–107, 110–111, 112, 152

Monique Dykstra, 75 (bottom)

John Fallis, i

Fred Gaskin, 19, 24 (bottom), 26

Tom Hall Photography, 57, 61 (bottom), 63

Sara Harrison, 40, 46

Antoni Harting, 32–33, 35, 36–37, 42–43, 45

Darcy Heath/University of Alberta, 53

Bill Ivy, 49

Pat and Rosemarie Keough, 123, 126, 127

Bill Mason, 80–81, 83, 86 (top), 86–87, 88 (bottom), 89, 91, 92, 114–115, 116–117, 120, 121, 124, 128–129

Parks Canada, 58 (bottom), 133

James Raffan, 13, 39 (top), 50–51, 54, 58 (top), 61 (top), 62, 85, 88 (top), 148–149, 150

William Reynolds, 39 (bottom)

Sandy Richardson, ii–iii, xvi, 17, 18, 23, 24 (top)

Kathleen Usher, 64–65, 67, 68–69, 70, 71, 72–73, 75 (top), 76–77, 78

Paul von Baich, 96–97, 100–101

Alan Whatmough, cover, 85